RANDOM
GOD
SIGHTINGS

RANDOM
GOD
SIGHTINGS

Kelly Hanes

Columbus Press
P.O. Box 91028
Columbus, OH 43209
www.ColumbusPressBooks.com

EDITORS
Brad Pauquette and Emily Hitchcock

ARTWORK, DESIGN & PRODUCTION
Columbus Publishing Lab
www.ColumbusPublishingLab.com

LCCN: 2019939680

Paperback ISBN: 978-1-63337-265-8
E-book ISBN: 978-1-63337-266-5

Printed in the United States of America
1 3 5 7 9 10 8 6 4 2

CONTENTS

Introduction   1

1: God Buys Lottery Tickets   7

2: God Is a Teacher   14

3: God Goes to the Doctor   21

4: God Plays Video Games   26

5: God Sees Specialness   33

6: God Sells Running Shoes   39

7: God Rides the Bus   46

8: God Is a Sick Girl   51

9: God Lives at Lowe's   55

10: God Is a Soldier   60

11: God Watches Chess Tournaments   65

12: God Sings   71

13: God Paints Nails   75

14: God Is an Old Woman   84

15: God Is a Nurse   89

16: God Is a Teenager   98

17: God Goes to Festivals   105

18: God Visits the Santa Shop   111

19: God Eats Doritos   119

20: God Is a Little Buddha   125

21: God Is a Greenbelt   134

22: God Studies Philosophy   145

23: God Is a Dog   153

24: God Is an Atheist   163

25: God Is a Boy   172

26: God Is a Mean Woman   177

Conclusion: It Begins   181

Epilogue to God Is a Sick Girl   183

AUTHOR'S NOTE

I refer to God in this book as He, and in a few cases, when it suits the Sighting, She. I also use the term "Father." The reader will understand that those are words that are comfortable for me. But of course, God is not He or She; He is Both and He is Neither. He is quite simply beyond the words of man…or woman.

It Begins
INTRODUCTION

Let it be simple, and it is.

BROTHER JAMES

THAT WHICH COMES EASILY holds very little value for us. We know very well that everything good, everything worth having, must be worked for, struggled for, *earned*. Industrious souls, we are forever pushing ourselves harder and harder to "take it to the next level." The next promotion, the next house, the next vacation, the next project, the next relationship—each one intended to be somehow bigger and better than the last. When the pushing, the striving, and the reaching leave us unsatisfied or restless, we turn our exhausted thoughts to God. Might He be there?

But as we begin to search for God, we bring the same pushing, striving, and reaching to our efforts to find *Him*. The next church, the next workshop, the next guest speaker or minister, the next meditation… We speak of journeys and paths, of learning lessons and finding missions. We find these helpful, we think we touch Him sometimes, but then He seems to slip away again, and the restlessness returns. It just isn't enough. It is never, ever enough.

As it turns out, as we work and struggle and strain, our tenderhearted Creator is showing up—Showing Up All Over The Place. We just don't see it because we are so wholly consumed by our efforts to push, to strive, to reach. Quite simply, when we operate from the mindset that seeing God or feeling His presence is difficult and involves much hard work on our part—and even at its best it will be only a fleeting experience—we are at odds with The Truth. The Truth is, you don't work hard to *earn* seeing God. He doesn't want that. He never did.

I know all about it. I had learned to live with the wondering and the wandering, the reaching and the *working hard* to learn all my lessons. I was sometimes full of joy, but I was more often filled with pain and the by now all-too-familiar restlessness that seemed to insist that there must be Something More. I must do better, I must get it right, I must attend this workshop, read this book, listen to this speaker…and it would all begin again.

And then one day, when I wasn't straining or pushing, at a time when I was living the smallest of lives in the smallest of places, going about the business of my day, I discovered something re-markable. God had been seen in the local convenience store. He bought a lottery ticket, and then He gave it away. No one won the lottery that week, but a life was changed, all the same.

I couldn't shake it. I couldn't stop thinking about God visiting a clerk in a gas station convenience store. After hearing the story, I allowed myself to wonder about God showing up randomly when we least expect it. *What if it's true?* I asked myself. *What if He really does show up randomly, when we least expect it?*

The question stayed with me, nagged at me, whispered to me, and my curiosity grew until finally I decided to conduct an experiment. I intended to find out if God was showing up in other places, just like He did that day in the convenience store. *God*, I would say at the beginning of each day, *I'd like to see You today*. Making the request made me feel like my experiment was *real*, like I was taking it seriously. And just in case He was listening, I wanted God to know that I was taking it seriously too. Remembering to ask became part of my early morning ritual.

It seems that asking is all that is required, for that simple re-quest served as a catalyst for a series of experiences that changed my life forever. I started seeing God. Randomly. When I least ex-pected it. After a while, He began speaking to me as well. And my life has never been the same.

Life is so much better when you see God every day. Life becomes joy-filled. You become happier, healthier, and more creative. Problems start smoothing themselves out. Projects seem to click, to flow. You worry less and laugh more. And why not? After all, God is here! After a while, you also start remembering Who You Really Are and why you're here, and that is the best part of all.

Gilbert Fowler White wrote that Albert Einstein once said, "There are only two ways to live your life. One is as though nothing is a miracle. The other is as though everything is a miracle." You are about to find out that everything is a miracle. Like the young woman in the convenience store who gave in to the impulse to tell me her story, I am giving in to the impulse to tell you mine. I want you to see what I see, to know what I know:

You are surrounded by miracles.

This book is designed to encourage you to read one story a day (only one!) for twenty-six days as you conduct your own experiment. The stories in this book are true. They serve as suggestions, possibilities; they are intended to give you examples of where you might see God and how it might feel—but your journey will be uniquely yours. You may read a story about a teacher and have a Sighting that involves a cashier. You may read a Sighting about an old woman and have a memory about a child spring forth. Your Sightings will be perfectly suited to *you*. In other words, I don't presume to change your life with *my* stories; my intention is that you change your life with *yours*. You're not going to come to understand that God is showing up in your life because of what I write, you're going to come to KNOW that God is showing up in your life because you are going to SEE it for yourself.

Sightings twenty-five and twenty-six are placed at the end of the book. They are to be read in order, one each day, during the final two days of your experiment. The other Sightings may be read in order, or randomly, as you see fit.

It's important to read only one story a day. This is an experiment, remember? A rushed experiment will not bring about valid results. Read one story each day, make your request to See God, and then simply allow your day to unfold…bringing to you as its gift your *own* Random God Sighting.

The stories in this book are small stories, and this is their gift. Let the smallness of the stories remind you that there is no life too small for His attention. Let them emphasize for you that there is no special preparation, no special place to go—that *He* comes to *you*, wherever you are, whatever your circumstances. And remember, "bigger is better" was *our* idea, not His. Your Random God Sightings may proceed gently. Your experiences may be small at first, subtle. An expression. A smile. A look in someone's eyes. But something inside you will stir and you will wonder. And if the wondering whispers, *"God, is that You?"*

It is.

Does this seem naive? Good. Sound childlike? Even better. "The kingdom of God belongs to such as these," the Teacher once said. Ask like a child and receive like a child. This is all you need to do. Begin each day with these simple words: "God, I would like to see You today," and then wait with an open, curious mind and a happy, expectant heart. For He will come. He always does. And your life will never be the same.

You can begin right now. Go ahead. Ask.

He's waiting for you.

GOD BUYS LOTTERY TICKETS

Joan: You are not real!
God: So people keep telling me.

JOAN OF ARCADIA

SHE GRITTED HER TEETH as she pulled the money out of the drawer, her jaw muscles visibly tightening, then forced a stiff smile as she counted out the change, careful to not make eye contact. If she made eye contact, they might see. See the despair. It was her own business, her despair. They had no right to it.

They filed in and out endlessly, the mothers with their SUVs and minivans, the fathers with their trucks. Teenagers in cool slick cars, or beat-up old ones. Teachers and bankers, secretaries, clerks and nurses—even the school bus drivers bought their fuel here. They bought their fuel and their Cokes and their cigarettes and their pain reliever—and of course, their lottery tickets.

Most of these people were in a hurry. If she wasn't fast enough, The Hurried Ones were sure to let her know with huffs and snorts, with an exasperated sigh or a roll of the eyes, with restless shifting from foot to foot or the click-click-click of well-manicured nails on the counter.

"Thank you. Come again."

She said it automatically, remembering too late that she was supposed to sound cheerful. That's what Jim, the manager, said, anyway. Gotta be cheerful. Customers want that.

She tried not to think about how tired she was or how much her feet hurt. She tried not to think about how, even with the extra hours, her paycheck was not going to be enough this week.

She glanced up briefly to check for her next customer. "Gas today, sir?" she prompted.

"No, ma'am. Not today."

Something about his voice caught her attention, and she looked up quickly from the cash register to take a closer look at his face, her fingers remaining poised to punch-punch-punch.

The old man stood there quietly. He placed nothing on the counter; he held nothing in his hands. He did not demand directions or ask in a loud voice where they kept the aspirin these days. He just stood there, looking at her, his gaze intense, probing. Then he smiled at her, gently.

Searching the old man's face, she thought he seemed familiar somehow. Perhaps he had been in the store before?

"Gonna buy a lottery ticket today, sir?" she suggested, smiling shyly.

"I don't buy lottery tickets," the man remarked simply, but not unkindly. "I never have."

Crap. She had forgotten again. She wasn't supposed to ask about the tickets. Jim said some folks in town were real religious—they thought gambling was a sin and that the lottery was gambling. So she wasn't supposed to *ask*.

With an anxious glance over her shoulder to see if Jim had heard her from his position at the other register, she apologized in a quick rush. "Oh, I am so sorry. I thought you were someone else."

But the man simply smiled again, his sky-blue eyes never leaving her face.

"Well, now," he said slowly, regarding her thoughtfully as he leaned forward to place a hip against the counter and fold two strong arms across a broad chest. "Just how much is the lottery up to this week?"

The girl nervously stammered out the figure. The man just stood there, looking at her with the bluest eyes (and whitest hair!) she'd ever seen, a trace of a smile still playing about his lips. He stood there as if there were no line of impatient customers behind him, as if he didn't hear the indignant sighs and the mur-murs of protest.

Something inside the girl began to soften, to relax. She was encouraged by the look in his eyes and wished to hold him there, if only a little longer. She ventured, with a deliberate grin this time that she hoped would show that she was teasing, "Just remember, if you buy one and win, you have to split it with me!"

As they looked at each other, the man and the girl, it seemed to the girl as if time stood still. She felt as if something airy and fresh was moving through her, and she imagined she saw lights in the man's eyes that seemed to shift and change. He was looking at her so kindly, looking at her like she was something special.

Sort of loving-like, she thought, marveling that a stranger could look at her like that.

The old man broke the silence. "I think I'll play the lottery today," he remarked casually. "Yes. I'll buy a ticket." He laid two dollar-bills on the counter. "Just one."

The girl pretended not to hear the exasperated, "Well, thank God!" muttered from the back of the line as she swiftly completed the transaction and handed the man his ticket. The old man nod-ded his head, just once; then reaching out, he gently took her hand in his and pressed the ticket into it.

"Here," he said. "It's yours. If you win, you can split it with me." With one last smile—this one radiant, like the sun—he left.

Tears filled her eyes and threatened to spill down her cheeks, but she dashed them away quickly to take the next customer's money. She felt lighter, almost happy. She couldn't explain it, but she felt that in some way the man had something to do with it. She cast a hopeful glance out the window as she handed the next customer her change, but the old man was nowhere in sight. It was only then that she realized that the ticket—she had hastily thrust it under the cash register—was the only item the man had purchased.

• • • • •

When you live in a rural community, "errand day" always includes an emergency stop so someone can use the bathroom. By the time you drive all the way into town and stop at a few places to pick up a few things, someone is inevitably crying out from the back seat, "Mooommmmyyyy! I…gotta…potty."

This errand day was no exception.

Once again, I found myself in the convenience store portion of the local gas station, waiting for my youngest daughter to come out of the restroom. I was engaged in another traditional part of errand day—the Selection of the Chocolate Bar. (The Chocolate Bar is the reward for running the errands.)

"The strangest thing happened today," announced the cashier from her position behind the counter.

Is she talking to me? I wondered. I glanced around to see if anyone else had entered the store. We seemed to be alone. *Odd*, I thought, *to be empty this time of day*. I returned my gaze to the young woman and looked at her expectantly, thinking as I looked at her that she looked a little tired around the eyes.

"An old man came in today," the woman began.

She hesitated as she looked at me, her head cocked slightly to one side, as if debating whether to continue. I smiled politely.

Just then my daughter joined me, slipping her hand into mine. The woman dropped her gaze to the little head at my side. My daughter briefly searched my face, then turned her regard to the woman, leaning her small body against mine. That seemed to decide it.

Smiling down at my daughter's upturned face, the woman proceeded to tell me the story about the old man and the lottery ticket. As she finished, she pointed to a ticket peeking out from underneath the cash register. I glanced at it, then back at the woman, and what I saw on her face caused me to catch my breath.

There were tears in her eyes as she gazed out the window—as if still looking for the man—and the expression on her face was soft and wondering. I felt goose bumps raise over my arms as I looked at her face.

It's almost as if God Himself came in here today to pay her a visit, to keep her going…

I knew that the woman was not going to win the lottery, but I understood from the faraway look on her face that it was not the winning that mattered.

"That's a great story," I managed awkwardly. "Thanks for telling me."

My chocolate bar forgotten, my daughter and I left the store. As I walked slowly toward the minivan, maintaining a firm grip on my daughter's hand so she could hop-hop-hop gleefully over mud puddles, the image of the woman's face lingered before me.

With a sigh, I remarked, half to myself and half out loud, "Wouldn't it be cool if God did that? Just showed up randomly when we least expected it?"

I was jolted from my reverie by my daughter's cheerful response.

"Maybe He does, Mommy. Maybe He does."

Maybe He does.

Sighting Two
GOD IS A TEACHER

I am not a teacher, but an awakener.

ROBERT FROST

WE LIVE IN A KILLING WORLD, and there are so many ways to kill. We live in a world where a terrorist can take the head of another human being to get media attention, where a boy can drive by in a car and shoot a person standing on the curb to prove his worth to his friends, where a man can sink a knife into another man's chest to avenge an infraction of an insane honor code. We live in a world where soldiers kill soldiers, where bombs kill the innocent, and criminals kill random prey. We live in a world where employees kill coworkers, where husbands kill wives, and where teenagers enter high schools and kill other teenagers. We kill for reasons, and we kill for no reason. We just kill.

These are not the only ways we kill, they are simply the most brutal and the most visible. For our world is not solely interested in killing the body, our world is also invested in the business of killing the soul, and it is here that we have become remarkably adept. Those of us who would never kill a body give little thought to killing someone's spirit. We kill spirits with our words, with our actions, with our whispered confidences—we kill with our very thoughts. We make killing decisions about each other. He is a loser. She is a slut. He will never stay sober and she will never stay clean. She's a bad mother. That child will never amount to anything. That teacher needs to retire. That doctor is an arrogant bastard. That man is a cheat...

You are mean. You are lazy. You are selfish. You are ugly. You are stupid. There isn't one of us who hasn't been caught up in the insanity at one time or another—some of us more often than others—caught up in the insanity of the killing world. And even those who labor tirelessly for The Other World, remembering always that they are members of Another Kingdom and must not lose heart, *even they* will raise their weary heads in an honest moment and tell you that, yes, it is a killing world we live in after all.

Yet, embedded within the killing world is another world, a world forever connected to The Good Kingdom, a world that each one of us has known. It stands as our reminder.

It is a world filled with laughter and shouts, with running, jumping, and cartwheels, with swinging and sliding and climbing; a world where restlessness is not reproached but celebrated. Runners halt near trees to become climbers, swingers jump out of swings—at the high end of the arc, of course—to become sliders, cartwheelers land with an exaggerated flourish before joining rope jumpers; and over and again leaders become followers become leaders become followers as one "fun" idea is exchanged for another.

It is not solely the world of movement, the celebration of the physical. It is also the world in which little creators first try their hands at creation. Thick, industrious little hands build structures with dirt and stones and sticks; slender, graceful hands draw pictures on the blacktop. If you don't give them chalk, they'll simply scratch it out with stone. Lovers of rhythm work out chants for the voice and arrange dances for the body; storytellers weave stories for rapt audiences, and comedians test out new jokes on easy-to-please crowds.

It is true that in this little world there are sometimes acts of unkindness or cruelty. But this world contains peacemakers as well. Already filled with a sense of mission, these little helpers move through their activities alert, ready to serve, to intercede, to create what *they* most love to create—peace. In this world, it is "wrong" to hurt another person. There is no gray, there is no maybe, there are no exceptions. The little peacemakers will explain this with unfaltering patience, yet unyielding firmness, as many times as it takes. They won't ask why you did it; the peacemakers already know.

In this world, conversations are shared, secrets exchanged, and broken hearts are exposed for healing as children go about the business of…Life. Life As It Should Be.

This is the world that we know and love before we forget.

• • • • •

As the sun moved in and out of ominous gray clouds threatening rain that restless March morning, I paused on impulse near the school playground to watch that little world in action, to marvel at its ebb and flow, its ease. As I watched the movement and the joy, heard the shouts and the laughter, I noticed a thin little girl in denim overalls, two brown braids halfway down her back, flanked on both sides by "helpers." She was limping. My first impulse was concern, but when I saw her awkwardly favoring first the left foot, then the right, I smiled to myself and continued to watch the girls as they slowly worked their way across the playground. It was one of those moments when time stands still. There was only the girls, and me watching the girls. Everything else fell away.

The helpers were attempting to support their injured friend

by placing her arms across their shoulders, imitating the grownups they had seen in the movies and on TV. Their heads were bent closely to hers, their faces full of care and concern, and there was much animated conversation.

On the limping victim's right was a stout little helper, solidly built. The helper was flushed and sweating with her exertion, her blond bangs damp on her forehead, the rest of her lank hair clinging to the sides of her face and the back of her neck. Her brow was puckered and her expression was earnest as she advised her patient. Support from the left was supplied by an energetic, wiry little girl with short black hair that seemed to stick straight out of her head in exuberant defiance of any attempt to create a "style." Her expression was less serious than that of the stout little helper. Helper Number Two had the look of a cheerleader—coaxing, coaching, encouraging. Go-Fight-Win.

Then, looking across the playground, I saw the teacher.

She stood motionless beneath a big oak tree, shoulders square, posture erect. Her short-sleeved, pastel sweater had a metallic thread running through it. The sweater seemed to shimmer in the shifting sunlight that was present one moment, then not, as the clouds worked their way slowly across the sky. Her straight navy skirt fell smoothly to the middle of her calves. Her hair, short and gray, lay as obediently as her skirt, feathering neatly along the sides of her head, tapering to the back of her head. Only her bangs stirred, just a little, in the breeze. Her hands were quietly folded in front of her. In the little world of shouts and movement, the very air around her seemed calm and serene. Something about her posture, the stillness, the tree…thoughts of That Other Teacher tumbled into my mind, and I instinctively moved a step or two closer.

I looked closely at the teacher's face, and following her gaze, I realized that she was watching the girls, her dark eyes thoughtful, her face very still; and it seemed to me, from just across the way, that her expression was one of infinite patience and profound tenderness. I felt a tightness pass over me like the tension you feel before you cry. I was mesmerized, unable to look away from that face, and it occurred to me amidst the confused jumble of thoughts in my mind that it was not the face itself that was so remarkable, but rather, what the face was *expressing* that was moving me almost unbearably.

Suddenly, the sun burst out from behind a large cloud, flooding the playground, the teacher, and myself with light, and as it did so, it was as if That Other Light burst into my clouded mind as well. I understood why I felt like weeping, why I could not look away from her face…

It was God's face.

It was God standing there under that big oak tree in the little world of the playground, overseeing His little creators as they went about the business of Life. It was God watching His girls with such tenderness—two experiencing what it feels like to help someone in need, and one experiencing what it feels like to know that help is always near. It was God watching His children go about the business of Life—Life as it should be.

It was God's face, revealed to me in the face of The Teacher.

Sighting Three
GOD GOES TO THE DOCTOR

Love is a fruit in season at all times,
and within the reach of every hand.

MOTHER TERESA

SOMETIMES THE NEWS IS GOOD. Sometimes the news is bad. Sometimes you think bitterly that you can't believe what you've been reduced to, what you'd be willing to accept as good news. Your heart aches for your child as you sit there waiting, but before long, the ache begins to grow and you are aching for the other children as well—and their mothers, fathers, and grandparents. You look at the young parents with their anxious expressions and fear-filled eyes, still clinging to desperate hope that the news may yet be good. You look at the older parents—the parents whose news was never as good as they had hoped—with their determined expressions and their fierce, courageous eyes. You watch the healthy siblings patting, encouraging, reading, or just keeping quiet company.

In the end, you don't know whom you ache for most…

• • • • •

I was in the neurologist's office of Children's Medical Center with my young son, the waiting room now behind me, watching the nurse take his blood pressure near the nurses' station. His twin sister stood at my side, silent, watching. I heard a door open and the sound of voices, and I turned to see two women and a little boy come out of one of the examining rooms into the hallway. I scanned the women quickly, automatically. *Mother and daughter*, I thought, as I noted the difference in the women's ages. Grandma had come along to help today.

In fact, it was Grandma's booming voice that had caught my attention. Her body matched her sound, large and commanding. She was wide with thick limbs—grossly overweight, obese—but somehow she conveyed strength and power instead of excess. Her daughter, the boy's mother, blond and immaculately dressed, makeup flawless, was thin, too thin. Her slight body did not convey Grandma's power. Still, there was a wiriness to her build that suggested a latent endurance. But it was the boy who caught my full attention. His mother held him in her arms like a baby, although his body had long ago stopped being the body of a baby. He lay limp in his mother's arms, completely and profoundly still, mouth gaping open, eyes glazed over, staring vacantly at the ceiling.

He must be heavy for her, I thought, tears springing to my eyes.

Grandma's voice startled me as she asked her daughter curtly in her loud voice, "Do you want me to hold him?" I ventured a peek at Grandma's face, and I noted that her eyes belied the harshness of her tone, eyes that anxiously searched the face of the thin, quiet daughter who stood beside her.

Her daughter answered her softly, "I guess. If you want to."

They exchanged the boy swiftly and efficiently in the practiced manner of those who had done it many times before.

Suddenly, the boy, lying motionless in his grandmother's arms, made a strange gurgling noise. It was disturbing. I glanced at my eight-year-old twins' faces to see their barely disguised alarm and distaste. I shot them a warning glance and looked back to see the mother dabbing the boy's tracheotomy tube with a Kleenex to absorb the bubbling secretions. Her lips were pursed together tightly, turning down at the ends; she could barely suppress *her* distaste at the fluids draining from her child. But her hands, her perfectly manicured hands, were very gentle. And the massive arms of the stern-faced grandmother, bare in her sleeveless blouse, cradled the boy tenderly.

Oh, God! My heart cried out in bitter accusation to my unseen Creator, *I don't understand You! How could You...*

But my accusation stopped midstream, and time once again stood still as my gaze was caught by a sudden shift in the light. I looked at the boy's face. Was there Something there? I blinked, deliberately, and looked again. The boy's body remained utterly still, eyes staring blankly at the ceiling, yet I could almost swear there was a light streaming forth from his face. And in that light, the expressions on the faces of the mother and grandmother were transformed. As they looked down at the motionless boy in Grandma's arms, their faces were beautiful, gentle, full of tenderness, and they were smiling at him.

There was a Great Force present. I could feel It as if It were tangible. I felt as if It were touching everyone in that room, running right through us. What was It? Where was It coming from? In that moment I realized that "It" was emanating from the boy, but it was somehow part of the women as well. It was one huge, unifying Force, and It was touching *me*. I stood there, stunned, my unseen Creator no longer unseen.

I came to with a start, finding myself seated in the examining room with no memory of getting there. The nurse was looking at me expectantly, tapping her pen absently on my son's open chart. I realized that she had asked me a question and was waiting for an answer.

"I'm so sorry," I stammered. "I know you see it all the time. But those people out there…"

The nurse shook her head and sighed with downcast eyes. "I know," she said. "So sad."

I looked at her blankly for a moment, but I said nothing. I said nothing because I didn't know how to say it. I didn't know how to tell her that I had just seen God in the hallway.

But I had.

Sighting Four
GOD PLAYS VIDEO GAMES

He only fears men who does not know them,
and he who avoids them will soon misjudge them.

Die Menschen furchtet nur, wer sie nicht kennt
Und wer sie meidet, wird sie bald verkennen

JOHANN WOLFGANG VON GOETHE,
TORQUATO TASSO (I, 2, 72)

WE LIVE IN DANGEROUS TIMES, and we live every day knowing it. There are bad people in the world, people who will hurt us—or worse, hurt our children—if we give them the chance. We live on guard, ever watchful, fiercely determined that the bad people will never be given the chance to hurt our children, and we try not to think too much about how wrong it all is. Sometimes, though, sitting in small groups at a ball game, or having lunch with friends, or at work discussing a news story about a recent abduction, we allow ourselves to talk about it a little. We share with each other our horror that we, who as children roamed freely through the neighborhood, needing only to "be home by dark," can never allow our children to do the same. We, who were chased out of the house by parents with orders to get some fresh air and sunshine, cannot simply send our own children out to play. We, once free to hop on bikes and ride all over town on a long summer day, sometimes alone, sometimes with friends, must explain carefully to our children that they can never be alone, never enjoy the solitary pleasure of their own company, but rather must always practice the buddy system.

No, if our children want to play, *arrangements* must be made with parents who will be present and for yards that will have fences. Even then, we worry that perhaps the parents are not as "safe" as they seem, and we worry about teenagers in the home. What might they do to our children? We minimize the amount of time our children are allowed to play outside of our presence. We carefully scrutinize the people they will be with and the places we allow them to go, and when we *do* allow them to go, we anxiously press cell phones into their hands, insisting that they call often to "check-in and let us know you're okay." When they return, we drill them with questions about "what they're like over there" to better prepare ourselves for future invitations to play. We sometimes feel guilty for our anxious thoughts concerning people we sense are most likely good, but the thoughts come anyway, seemingly of their own accord. We live in dangerous times, after all.

We teach our children about the dangers of this world with

awkward phrases and sad rhyming words. We speak of "stranger danger," of "good touches" and "bad touches." And looking into their questioning eyes, watching the confusion, the alarm, and finally the fear and uneasiness reflected there, we feel physically ill. We hate what we've had to say, hate what we've had to make them think. But we have no choice. We live in dangerous times. The children grow older, but the phrases and words remain awkward. We speak of date rape and abduction and murder and unspeakable acts. "Unclean! Unclean!" cry our weary spirits, but we grit our teeth and we do it. To do otherwise would be bad parenting. We live on guard, watchful and anxious, ever aware that we live in dangerous times...

• • • • •

I was at the local grocery store, waiting my turn in the checkout aisle, when the twins asked me if they could go look at the video game machines in the small lobby. My children's intention, when they make this seemingly innocent request, is twofold: one, to check the machines, and the dirty floor, for forgotten quarters (they never give up hope), and two, to watch for someone with quarters to spend (they are a rapt audience for anyone trying to win a stuffed animal from the robotic game.) As I hesitated, debating, Big Brother (two years their senior) offered to go along and take care of them. I said yes…reluctantly. *It should be fine*, I announced firmly to the slight knot in my stomach as I watched them run off. But we live in dangerous times, the knot remained, and I hurried through the line to join them as quickly as possible.

As I entered the lobby, my children rushed to greet me. All three of them were beaming, jumping up and down, waving stuffed animals in the air. "Where did you get that money?" I hissed. (I usually do not allow my children to spend their own quarters—or mine—trying to win stuffed animals from grocery store machines like "The Claw.")

Today, even as I scolded, I puzzled, *What's going on here? All three? There's no way.*

The children proceeded to tell me, all laughing and talking at once, that a man had given them the stuffed animals. The knot in my stomach returned. Interrupting them I asked, "You mean the vendor? The man who fills the machine?"

No, no, they told me, just a man. He wins animals and gives them away to kids, they insisted. Why, he had just left when I entered the lobby, they said. Just. Left.

Not the vendor? I rolled it over in my mind. *And why did he leave at my approach?* As we stepped from the lobby out into the parking lot, my children became animated once again, pointing out the man just across the way. Something uneasy rippled through me at the sight of him, and the knot in my stomach tightened. I ordered the children into the minivan and admonished them to wait there. I locked the doors and set off across the parking lot, visions of the next day's headlines flashing through my mind. "Local Woman Apprehends Child Molester"; "Mother of Four Thwarts Abduction Attempt." I caught up quickly and reached the man just as he was preparing to unlock his van. The van was white, but so old and beaten up that it looked almost gray. There were scratches on the sliding door of the driver's side and a nasty dent in the rear bumper. There were no cheerful graphics decorating the van—no pictures advertising plumbing services or flower delivery or in-home computer repair—nothing to explain its worn condition.

And the windows were *tinted*.

*Oh! A **van!*** said the cold little voice in my head. I felt uneasiness flush over me as the man looked up to see me standing there.

"Why, I…" I floundered.

Pretend to thank him! suggested the voice brightly.

"Well, you see," I continued, "my children tell me that you gave them stuffed animals just now. I thought perhaps you were the vendor?" I shifted my weight to my right foot as I spoke, attempting to get a glimpse of the inside of his van. "And I just… well…wanted to…um…thank you."

"No, ma'am. I'm not the vendor," the man replied quietly. I looked at him. He was an older man, solidly built and tan—not the tan of a tourist but the tan of a farmer, deep-baked and hard-earned, just like the deep furrows in his brows and the wrinkles around his eyes. His eyes. I looked into his eyes then, for the first time.

The cold little voice in my head began to falter. *He doesn't* **look** *like a child molester.*

"Well, I don't know what to say," I ventured. "I don't understand—"

"It's just somethin' I like to do, ma'am," he said kindly. He let out a soft laugh. "Turns out I'm good at those machines. I play 'em while my wife shops." He paused. "See, I…I miss my kids. My children are all grown now, and they've moved far away." He looked away, squinting in the sun as if looking to some far-off place, then turned his attention back to me and smiled. He shrugged. "Doin' this, winnin' the animals and givin' 'em to the kids, it makes me feel good. I come once a week. Usually on Thursdays."

I felt strangely unnerved, shaken.

"Not too many kids today," he noted, and I heard the soft note of disappointment in his tone. The man looked away again, just for a moment, before turning to look at me again. He smiled and said, "So I'm real glad yours came along when they did." He paused, contemplating me thoughtfully, then added, "They're good kids."

My heart began to pound. When he looked at me like that, wrinkles crinkling, dark brown eyes shining as he mentioned my children, it all washed through me…God! I was speaking with God in the middle of the grocery store parking lot, and God had been glad to see my children that day. Cheeks burning with shame for my earlier thoughts, I thanked the man for his kindness to my children…awkwardly, but this time with feeling.

I returned to my van, lost in thought, and climbed into the driver's seat. As I fastened my seatbelt, my eight-year-old son remarked brightly from his seat behind me, "You know what, Mom? People like that could change the world."

I almost let out a good-natured laugh and a teasing remark about the stuffed animals, but as I glanced into the rearview mirror, I swallowed it all at the sight of my son's expression. It was beautiful beyond words. And I realized in that moment, looking at my son's face, that he wasn't thinking about the stuffed animal. My son understood all about the man.

My son had seen God.

Oh, God, I thought, in a burst of gratitude. *Thank You so much.*

I felt my spirit lift.

Oh, um, and sorry for thinking You were a child molester.

I felt Laughter ripple through me. I joined it, laughing out loud.

Sighting Five
GOD SEES SPECIALNESS

We don't see things as they are;
we see them as we are.

ANAÏS NIN

THEY CHATTER AT THEIR TABLES, in between bites of chicken nuggets, macaroni, or pizza, exchanging stories about sports heroes, video games, cousins and cartoons and movie stars. They will tell you things if you sit quietly. They will tell you that Grandpa is coming home from the hospital today but now he needs a cane; that Mommy says she's fat and threw out all the junk food and the whole family has to eat healthy now; that Stepdad taught them how to hold the bat "the right way" last night. They'll tell you that Daddy lost his job, and Mommy cried and said, "What will we do for money?" They'll tell you that little sister threw up three times in one night, and that big brother listens to music with bad words.

They're sad about the divorce, worried that their loved ones will die, and they think their pets are very funny. In other words, they talk about Life.

They require very little participation when they're telling a story; they do, however, require that you indicate your rapt attention from time to time with widened eyes, a sympathetically murmured, "Oh, Honey," an enthusiastic "For Heaven's Sake!" or a sincere "Really?"

They are second-graders.

• • • • •

I was sitting in the school cafeteria having lunch with a table of second-graders, listening to their stories. After one particularly energetic storyteller finished telling an elaborate story about a recent accomplishment, I remarked, my tone indicating the appropriate enthusiasm, of course, "Wow, I bet that made you feel special!"

Rats. I realized my mistake the minute the words were out of my mouth. I had used the "S" word.

Immediately they all clamored, as second-graders always do:

"I'm special too!"

"Hey, I'm special!"

"What about me? Do you think I'm special?"

Rushing to reassure them, I said in my best Wise-and-Knowing voice, "*Of course* you are special. In fact, I have special eyes that can see people's specialness, and I can see that *everyone at this table* is special." There was a pause while they considered my proclamation. Satisfied, they resumed their conversations.

Crisis averted, I thought wryly.

She sat across the table from me, a little girl with thick brown hair that flowed in waves over her shoulders, down her back and all the way to her waist. Her brown eyes were huge and thoughtful. She was a quiet girl, a straight-A student who never caused her teacher a moment's frustration. When mothers asked their children what this girl was like, their children invariably responded with an "Oh! She's *nice*." The pronouncement was usually followed by a story illustrating an act of kindness on the girl's part. "She gave me her pink pencil with the sparkles when I lost mine. She said I could keep it." "She helps Travis on his papers." "She told Brittany to stop being mean to Kara." Nevertheless, the children knew very little about her outside of her acts of assistance. She did not tell stories or engage in chatter. She had only two close friends with whom she ate lunch and played at recess. If she spoke, it was to them. What she spoke about, no one but those two girls knew.

This day was going to be different.

The quiet girl turned huge, solemn brown eyes upon me and said resolutely, "I can see people's specialness." She had made a statement, but I had the strangest feeling I was being asked a question. The girl was watching me closely for my reaction, her expression commanding my full attention. I sensed I was being tested somehow.

My thoughts scrambled in my head. What was she hoping I'd say? Did the child see auras? Of course, one does not discuss auras or angels or even God in the public school system. I certainly knew *that*. The parents would complain to the principal and demand that he *do* something, and the principal would have to "speak" with me—firmly. It was an unpleasant business all around. Yet, there she sat, expectant, waiting for my response. She waited calmly, patient-ly, as if she had time…all the time in the world.

What could I say to this child that would encourage her, but also be acceptable to today's parents? There wasn't much. So I smiled and said simply, in a tone that I hoped sounded sincerely respectful, "Really? That is a wonderful thing."

Somehow, it was enough. Her little body relaxed as she smiled in return, a broad, easy smile now, and she pointed to a thin little girl across the table a few seats down.

"Like her," she said. "Right now. I can see her specialness coming out of her."

She pointed just over the little girl's shoulder. "There," she said, "and there," pointing over the other shoulder. "And there and there." I followed the movement of her graceful arm, the direction of her slender index finger, and nodded my head thoughtfully, wondering all the while, *What does this child see?*

Even more curious, she was pointing to the most "difficult" child in the class, a scrawny little wisp of a girl who marched—rather, stomped—to the beat of her own drum, irritating everyone in the class in the process. *She* had no friends at all, the teacher would sigh with resignation, admitting reluctantly that it was hard to keep pushing the other children to be friendly to her when the girl wouldn't even *try* to get along, not even a little. Her classmates were often unkind in expressing their exasperation with her. The girl would only toss her blond hair and pretend not to care.

This day was going to be different.

I realized with a start that the entire table had become silent. I glanced to my right and to my left to discover all the children watching the difficult girl, each and every one of them looking at her intently, straining to see the specialness. No one protested. No one called out, "I don't see it!" Their trust in the brown-haired, brown-eyed girl was absolute. If *she* said it was there, then it must certainly be there. Their little faces were beautiful as they gazed at their difficult classmate, searching for her specialness.

Time stood still, and I felt a stillness creep over me as I watched them watching her.

As for the difficult girl, she sat wide-eyed, posture erect, her ever-restless body for once quiet and still. She lifted her chin and tilted her head just slightly, holding her head regally, like a queen. She was beaming, basking in the attention, as all her classmates looked upon her specialness in respectful silence. I have never seen a child look so happy, a face so full of joy.

The silence finally broke, and the children returned to their conversations. I looked at the brown-eyed girl and smiled, and she smiled back at me. It was then, in that moment, that I saw God, right there, in the girl's eyes. Shining, confident, exultant.

Oh, God! I said in my mind. *Is that You? I should have known!* I felt my heart lift, my spirit soar.

As we sat there looking at each other, God and I, one of Her classmates leaned over and confided to us, voice lowered, "You know what? Sometimes I think I see specialness too."

God sees Specialness.

There and there and there…

Sighting Six
GOD SELLS RUNNING SHOES

I always loved running...
It was something you could do by yourself,
and under your own power.
You could go in any direction, fast or slow as you wanted,
fighting the wind if you felt like it, seeking out new sights
just on the strength of your feet
and the courage of your lungs.

JESSE OWENS

THEY GLIDE BY, those lean, mean, running machines, every day at the same time without fail. Below zero or above ninety, weekday, weekend or holiday, soaking with rain or soaking with sweat, they breeze by, isolated by choice, a look on their faces that tells you their bodies are present but their minds are not as they call out their hellos. They don't compete in marathons and they don't run with friends. They just run. We call them "intense" or "fanatic" as they sail by, our arms wrapped around grocery bags or hands tugging at briefcases, and we mutter that they've gotten carried away with the whole thing. But deep down, as we watch their retreating backs disappear from view, we wonder about that faraway look on their faces…

• • • • •

For as long as I could remember, I longed to be one of those lean, mean, running machines. I wanted to feel what they felt. I wanted to know what they knew. I wanted my mind to go to those places the mind can only go after you're sixty minutes into the run.

I had a soul that wanted to run and a body that could not manage to do so. Occasionally I would enjoy some modest success. I would work my way up to a sixty-minute run, alone, my legs stretched out and strong, the fresh air filling my lungs, my spirit soaring. Like an excited child crying out to her parents when she first masters her two-wheeler without training wheels, I would cry out in my mind, *Look! I'm doing it! I'm doing it!* I was like *them*, those runners! Soon *I* would be a lean, mean, running machine too.

But try as I might, I was plagued with problems with my feet and lower legs. I tried ice, I tried heat. I tried rest, I tried running through the pain. I took Tylenol, I took Motrin. I read magazines, surfed the net and made appointments at sports medicine clinics. I even prayed for healing. Nothing helped, not even the praying. At long last, I was bitterly considering giving up.

So the last thing I wanted to do that sunny Saturday afternoon was shop for another person's shoes—a person who could run as he pleased and not have his lower legs scream in agony. That's what I needed to explain to my husband when he asked me to accompany him as he shopped for new shoes at The Finish Line. I hesitated as I searched my mind for the right words, trying to find a way to express myself that didn't sound resentful or selfish. Soccer season was approaching, he reminded me as I demurred, and he needed new shoes. I made a face at him. I pointed out that we'd never had any success in that kind of shoe store anyway. They're always staffed by Young Kids Who Don't Care. He wheedled, and I reluctantly agreed to go with him, my exasperation ill-disguised.

As my husband shopped for soccer shoes, I wandered over to the women's running shoes and gazed forlornly at all the shoes I would never wear on all the runs I would never take. A young man walked up and asked if he could help. Looking at him, I immediately thought how young he looked, and in the very next instant it occurred to me how *I* must look to *him*—just a dumpy housewife. I was about to mumble an embarrassed, hurried, "No thanks I'm just waiting on my husband," when instead, to my own surprise, I blurted out, "I just wish I could run!"

There was complete silence as he looked at me.

What are you doing, you idiot? demanded the cold little voice in my head. I felt foolish and began to mentally scramble for clever words to turn my outburst into some sort of lighthearted witticism that would comfortably dismiss the boy and send him on his way. I shifted slightly and turned my head to avoid looking at him directly. "Oh, I mean, uh…" I sputtered.

"What seems to be the problem?" he asked quietly.

Something in his tone caught my attention. There was something genuine in it, something sincere. It wasn't slick and practiced, nor was it indifferent and slightly bored. Turning to look at his face fully, I was surprised to find that the young man was looking at me attentively, earnestly.

I tried to refrain, but there was something about the look in the young man's eyes. The impulse that had first caused me to blurt my frustration took full control, and suddenly I was spilling out my years of struggle. *Oh, you have GOT to be kidding!* snickered the mean little voice in my head. But there was no stopping me. There I stood, the dumpy little woman, pouring out her dumpy little frustration to a young man who looked like he was the star of the local track team.

His manner was patient and his large blue eyes thoughtful; but when I finished, to my dismay, he remained silent. Oh, why had I done it? I'd made a fool of myself. Cheeks burning, I waited expectantly for him to make the usual token suggestions. They would be the same suggestions as always, I knew, and I would say, "No I've tried that but thank you," and that would be the end of it. I'd slink out, my humiliation complete, to wait for my husband on the bench outside.

Hands clasped quietly in front of him, head cocked slightly to one side, eyes never leaving my face, the young man did *not* make the usual token suggestions but instead proceeded to ask me a series of questions. He did not look away from me to check on the other customers, and his manner was gently encouraging as I stammered out my answers. He listened. I mean, Really Listened.

"Wait here," he finally said.

He returned with a pair of running shoes and a set of inserts. He smiled.

No! I cautioned myself sternly. *He's sweet to try, but you know nothing works. Don't you dare get your hopes up.*

The young man placed the inserts into the shoes, and then helped me get the shoes on. I stood up and my feet felt...different. My husband had wandered over to see what was going on, and I glanced up at him, becoming increasingly animated. "Ohmygosh!" I cried to him in a rush, already abandoning my self-admonishment not to hope. "I don't know what to say. I don't know—these feel different. I don't want to get my hopes up, but we may be on to something."

I looked back at the shoe salesman. His hands were folded again, and there was a stillness that seemed to be emanating from him…as if he had all the time in the world for this…all the time in the world *for me*. He was smiling again and his eyes were merry. For a split second I thought he was laughing at me, and I paused, prepared to be embarrassed at my display of excitement. But looking closely at his face, I realized that he was genuinely pleased.

"Are these new?" I demanded, pointing to the shoes and the inserts.

The young man answered that no, the inserts were not particularly new; they had been around for a while. The shoes? He shrugged cheerfully. Just something he thought we ought to try.

I was puzzled. "I don't understand!" I said impatiently. "All these years, all the stories I've told to so many shoe salesmen. Why hasn't anyone ever suggested these to me before?"

The boy answered slowly, pretending consideration. "Why…I don't know."

But in that instant, looking at the twinkle in his eyes, *I* knew, and the knowing made me burst into a smile of my own and then laugh out loud with delight.

You see, God understood all about the dumpy housewife who

longed to run. God understood that when she was running, she wasn't dumpy or overwhelmed by life. When she was running she was young and strong, brave and ready to take on the world. Yes, God understood it all. So just when she thought she would have to give it all up, God decided to sell running shoes.

God sells running shoes…and other things.

Sighting Seven
GOD RIDES THE BUS

When will our consciences grow so tender
that we will act to prevent human misery
rather than avenge it?

ELEANOR ROOSEVELT
"MY DAY," FEBRUARY 16, 1946

SHE'D HAD ENOUGH OF HIM. She really had. He was restless and relentless and she hated him. She fumed. Well, she'd fix him, she decided. She'd fix him but good.

"Guess what?" she announced loudly, with a shake of her pretty blond head. Her tone commanded the immediate attention of those nearby, for it promised that this was going to be good. Children halted conversations in order to listen. It was well known, and much celebrated, that she always had the most interesting things to say. Such clever, funny things. This would be good, they knew. It always was.

She scanned them quickly, assuring herself that she had secured their attention. The wait only increased their anticipation. A few more conversations were interrupted as the sudden diminution in noise caused others to realize that "something" was going on. Heads turned, and some of her fellow riders leaned out of their seats to better see her. At last pleased with the number of listeners, she moved quickly before they could lose interest. She "fixed" him with one small, powerful, seven-word declaration. In a very loud voice she called out to them all, "My brother peed the bed last night."

There was only a second of silence as the listeners took in the news. And in that second, the interrupted conversations were quickly forgotten, for this, indeed, was good. Very good. Her bus mates howled with laughter and the taunting began.

"Pee-pee pants, pee-pee pants."

"Bed wetter!"

"Baby! Baby! Baby! You need diapers."

He sat there, the younger brother, at first stunned and then horrified. He could barely take it in, but when he did, he thought that he might die. That's how bad he felt, bad enough to die. He shrunk down, trying to make himself smaller, trying to make himself disappear.

Ignoring a warning scowl from an older boy, the bus mates quickly spread the word throughout the entire bus. Children crowed with delight when they received the news, and after a quick glance to assure themselves the bus driver wasn't looking, they stood up or leaned out of their seats to get a better look at the bed wetter.

As the noise and the taunting grew, so did the boy's agony. There was no place to hide, wedged there between the bus window and his sister—his laughing, triumphant sister. Beside himself, the boy clutched his head in his hands and began to bang it against the side of the bus window, repeating slowly, over and over, like a litany, "I...hate...myself. I...hate...myself. I...hate...myself."

One seat away he sat, a thin, quiet, dark-haired boy. Two years older than the boy being taunted, but still younger than most of the children doing the taunting, he watched silently as the noise, and the little boy's agony, continued to build. The dark eyes missed nothing. The laughing, jeering faces with their twisted, cruel mouths. The look of triumph on the pretty sister's face. The ominous scowl from the older boy. But mostly, the crouched figure of the little boy, his small head, his sobbing litany. Finally, the dark-haired boy announced loudly enough for all to hear, "Don't worry about it, buddy. I peed the bed just last year!"

Once again, time stood still, and there was silence in the bus as the listeners considered what they had just heard.

And in that silence, the little boy slowly turned his head and lifted his eyes—for he had heard the announcement along with the others—and as green eyes met solemn brown from across the aisle, a light passed over his tortured face, his expression of sorrow exchanged first for wonder, then joy, as he beheld the face of his savior. His small hands released the hair they clutched and fell slowly from his head, coming to rest quietly on his thighs, and he became very still, his eyes never leaving the steady, dark-brown gaze turned upon him from across the aisle.

• • • • •

As my sons recounted this story to me one fine spring day, I thought to myself that this was a remarkable act of compassion coming from a young boy. But my stomach also knotted as I wondered what the consequences of the dark-haired boy's brave "announcement" had been. Expecting the worst, I turned quickly to my older son and demanded, "What happened next?"

"It was kind of weird, Mom," he said, cocking his head and raising an eyebrow. "There was a second or two where it was completely silent—the whole bus, Mom! Then you could sorta feel the energy shift…"

I held my breath and imagined myself there on the bus as my son described what followed the brief silence.

• • • • •

"Oh, yeah?" shouted a bus mate. "Well, I peed the bed just last week."

Giggles rippled through the bus.

"That's nothing," called out another. "I pee the bed every night!"

The entire bus erupted into peals of laughter, and the rest of the trip home was spent one-upping each other.

By the time the bus arrived home, the little boy who had been teased was laughing along with the rest. He hopped off the bus with an exaggerated jump and skipped up the driveway to his house with his sister. He was talking to his sister as he skipped, head tipped to the side to better see her. Her hand rested lightly on his shoulder as she laughed down at him, not with malice this time, but with restored good nature.

• • • • •

"The dark-haired boy?" I queried next.

My son shrugged. "He didn't say anything else, Mom."

The dark-haired boy's single sentence was the only one he uttered. He left the bus at his stop, his mission accomplished.

God rides the bus. Always.

Look for Him across the aisle.

Sighting Eight
GOD IS A SICK GIRL

It is a time when one's spirit is subdued and
sad, one knows not why; when the past seems
a storm-swept desolation, life a vanity and a
burden, and the future but a way to death.

MARK TWAIN

SITTING ON THE BLEACHERS at an indoor soccer game
that cold winter morning, I found myself grimly examining my
darkness. When had I become so downhearted and discouraged?
When had my life, as well as the world, begun to look so hopeless?
The future so bleak? What had been the trigger? When, exactly,
did it happen?

Do we ever know? Do we ever stop and say, "Oh, it is here,
it is now, that I enter the darkness?" I don't think so. We just one
day notice that we are there. And as to what put us there, does it
really matter? For we all go into the darkness sometimes, and the
reason is always the same...we are afraid. And left unattended,

51

the Fear begins to grow.

I looked up to see her standing at the net, watching the game. She was a slight little thing in her bib overalls, her fine brown hair flowing down her back. She was only twelve, and she had a brain tumor. The doctors would operate in three days. Her mother moved quietly through the stands from mother to mother, asking for prayers. They had received the results of the brain scan. The tumor had worked its ugly fingers through the entire brain and wrapped itself around the brain stem as well. There was little hope. The family was to prepare for the worst.

Unaware of her mother's activity, the girl stood at the net quietly, watching her little sister play ball. *So thin*, I thought, looking at her there. I felt a spasm clutch my heart, and I was consumed with sorrow. The world with all its darkness and suffering seemed to swirl around me, and there she stood. That it should claim her too…it was too much.

Something inside of me stirred, and my despair became a furious rebellion as I cried out to some unseen force, *No! Not this one! You will NOT have this one*. I laid thoughts of my own darkness aside, and I began to pray. Suddenly, in all the world there was nothing I wanted more than to pray for the little slip of a girl I saw at the net. The intensity of what I was feeling increased. I lost track of everything. I didn't hear the sounds of the game. I didn't see my son whiz by with the soccer ball. I saw only the girl. It was as if Time Stood Still.

Suddenly, the girl turned and looked at me. Fully. In the eyes. With several calm steps she approached me, her eyes never leaving my face. As she took a seat on the bleacher in front of me she said, "I think I will sit here for a while."

Her look and her remark were both unmistakably for me, and I was taken aback at this, for this child and I did not know each other. Looking down at her, a feeling stole over me, something that felt like a longing. I felt strangely drawn to the girl. Without thinking, I leaned forward ever so slightly. I heard myself saying gently, "Well. I am a good place to be."

She tilted her head, just a little, and searched my face intently. She said softly, "Yes. Yes. You are safe." And that child—that child I did not know!—laid her head upon my knees and wrapped her arms around my legs. And again, without planning to, I leaned over her and wrapped my arms around her thin little body and held her as she held me.

From a far-off place I could hear myself thinking, *You should pray for her now, while you're holding her.* But I couldn't. I couldn't think of words, and I couldn't "make pictures" in my head. There was only me holding her and her holding me. It was something beyond words or pictures…it was almost a state of being. Finally she stirred, and we parted as if on cue. She remained a while longer, her hand resting on my knee, my hand resting on her back. We did not speak. And then she rose and left me. As I watched her walk away, I slowly realized that a powerful healing had just occurred.

Mine.

My darkness was gone. Because She saw my soul and acknowledged it. Because She chose to "sit with me a while." Because She looked me in the eye and pronounced me good. And somehow, in doing so, She had dispelled my darkness and I became well. I realized, as the girl disappeared from my sight, that it was God who had laid Her head upon my knee and wrapped Her arms around me. And it was God I had held in my arms.

God is a sick girl, healing you.

* See Epilogue to "God Is a Sick Girl."

Sighting Nine
GOD LIVES AT LOWE'S

The reward of a thing well done,
is to have done it.

RALPH WALDO EMERSON

NOT TOO LONG AGO, I unwillingly accompanied my husband on a trip to Lowe's. I didn't want to go. I didn't want to go because, as all women know, a trip to Lowe's with a husband or boyfriend just to "pick up a thing or two" stretches out into infinity. The man's eyes become wide, and then glazed, and he has to touch everything. He wanders, wanders, wanders, mumbling things to himself that you can never understand. He doesn't hear you sigh, he doesn't see you look at your watch, and he doesn't even speak when you remark that you have to go to the bathroom. He just vaguely waves his free hand in the direction of the back of the building, unable to tear his eyes away from the power tool he's inspecting.

I've found the only way to accelerate the leaving process is to become very animated and start suggesting we buy everything we see. "How cool!" I cry out. "We need this! Let's get one!" "Oh, look! I need a bunch of these!" My personal favorite, the one designed to rocket me out of there at the speed of light: "*So what* if tile is more expensive? I don't care *how* much it costs. I want the very, very best!"

Despite my reluctance, I agreed to go that Sunday because, well, it was *Sunday*. I still retained, from my childhood days, the notion that Sundays were family days. Wives and husbands should be together on Sundays. It felt vaguely wrong to send him off on his own, especially when I knew he would be pleased if I accompanied him. Besides, I was out of sorts, and I worried that it might be lonely to stay back at the house alone, just me, myself, and my out of sortedness.

Five minutes into the store, however, I found myself frowning and listening with increasing impatience as my husband muttered about the things he was picking up and looking at. I. Felt. So. Annoyed.

Heaving a loud sigh, I happened to look up, way up, and I absentmindedly noticed how it *feels* in Lowe's. *The ceilings are high*, I thought, *and the aisles are wide. I like that. Makes a person feel like they can stretch out.* No crowding, no bumping into others, no need to make polite conversation as you both reach for the same thing.

Sort of soothing, I thought. *For a store, anyway.*

With a sigh I looked over at my husband to find that he had moved farther on down the aisle without a word to me. I glared at him as I drifted over to join him, knowing all along that he would remain utterly oblivious to my displeasure. As he wandered through the aisles, I followed silently, arms folded across my chest in an expression of protest.

I began to watch the people in the aisles as we wandered through, looking closely at their faces. Their attitudes were relaxed, unhurried. They seemed lost in thought. Like my husband, they touched everything. Sometimes their faces were filled with wonder, like a child's. They smiled absently, brows puckered as they examined first this, then that, and then held both to compare, intent upon their task, full of a bustling sort of energy. A few were with companions of like mind, to whom they would occasionally exclaim in short, excited, few-word bursts over some remarkable aspect of a particular item. The companion would enthusiastically agree, before both would return, each to his own search.

As I was watching a white-haired elderly man meticulously examine a screw, he happened to look up and catch me watching him. He nodded his head courteously, the old-fashioned way, and he smiled a gentle, sweet sort of smile. No rush. I smiled in return but quickly averted my gaze, uncomfortable at being caught staring, and the old man returned to the task at hand. But I had no sooner looked away than I felt the urge to look at the old man again, and I returned my gaze to his downturned face. There was something about the way he was examining the screws, how happy he seemed, how interested, how pleased. Looking at him, I caught myself wondering.

"God? Is that You?"

As if he heard my thoughts, the old man looked up at me again. He smiled at me, a warm and welcoming smile. I smiled in return, and this time did not avert my gaze. I felt Time Stand Still, and it was all I could do to keep tears from my eyes.

God was here, in Lowe's! I could *feel* Him. And I knew in that same instant *why* God was at Lowe's. Because His little creators were there! I caught my breath. I could almost imagine how much God loved His little creators at Lowe's, busy trying to be just like Him…trying to build, to create, to fix, to mend.

That's why everyone is so happy, I thought. *We're happiest when we're like Him*. The old man was still looking at me, and I had the strangest feeling that he knew my thoughts. He nodded, just once, almost as if to say, "Well done."

Once again, I had remembered! I had remembered Who

We Really Are, and now I was smiling at everyone as we walked through the aisles, hugging to myself the knowing, the remembering. God was here! And these were His children! The father with the long tangled hair and large eagle tattoo on his arm, giving his little daughter something to carry so she could "help"; the employee cheerfully coaching my husband, "I think what you want is over here…"; the people in the checkout lines, making room for each other, talking about their projects, laughing. I could feel God everywhere.

It's just like a church, I marveled.

Maybe better.

I think of God every time I go to Lowe's now. I think to myself, *This is God's house.*

Sighting Ten
GOD IS A SOLDIER

The most beautiful music of all
is the music of what happens.

IRISH PROVERB

WE SEE THEM IN OUR MALLS and on our downtown side-walks. Their bellies are round, but their legs remain perfectly shaped, their arms petite. Their hair is thick, their skin glowing, complexion flawless. Their eyes shine, and ours shine as well, thinking how we will look just like them when it is our turn, our turn to be "the little mother." Even those of us who say we don't want children, at least "not for a long time" because we have important career goals to achieve first—*even we* hold a secret place in our hearts for the time that we know will come, the time when we will walk, with bellies round but body perfect, full of joyful expectancy, buoyant confidence, basking in the warm smiles and kind glances the world showers upon us as the pretty little mother.

But then our turn finally comes, and our legs become swollen and our arms become heavy. We gain a shocking amount of weight, our hair becomes lank, and our skin breaks out like a teenager's or becomes discolored in odd patches. We are tired. We can't sleep. It is not at all what we expected. And one morning, staring dully in the mirror at a reflection we hardly recognize, a cold thought creeps into our troubled mind—what *else* won't be as we expected?

• • • • •

It was the beginning of May, and my first child was due at the end of the month. I had gained more than forty pounds and was retaining an alarming amount of water. Physically, I was miserable. Mentally, I was terrified. I longed to hold my firstborn child, but I was filled with anxiety as well. Something might go wrong. Maybe the baby wouldn't be okay. Deeper yet, I was afraid—afraid that I wouldn't be good enough. I'd restlessly read every new parent book I could get my hands on, but the little voice in my head nagged-nagged-nagged away, insisting that I would make mistakes, adding pointedly that they'd be big mistakes too.

Sitting in a rocking chair near my favorite window that sunny Saturday afternoon, crying with that special sort of abandon that marks a woman near their due date, I considered these disordered thoughts. The cold little voice in my head had reviewed all my faults, all my flaws, until finally I could only cry, *Enough! Enough!* and admit to myself that the little voice was right. It was a mistake. I shouldn't have done it. I was not fit to be a mother.

The doorbell interrupted my despair-filled thoughts, and wiping my eyes and nose, I lumbered to the door. I opened it to find a cheerful man waiting on the other side with a long white box. I knew all about long white boxes…long white boxes meant flowers. Maybe even *roses*. I was taken aback, but hopeful. For me? Was he sure? The cheerful man grinned, double-checked the address on the card, and said that he was sure.

Beaming, I snatched the box from his hands quickly, lest he check again and discover they weren't mine after all. "Oh, thank you! Thank you so much!" I cried emotionally, as if he himself were the generous giver. He chuckled and shook his head. As I watched his back recede down the stairs of my front porch, I fancied I heard him murmur something about pregnant women and hormones; but I was far too excited to be insulted.

Closing the door, I moved as quickly as my cumbersome frame would allow to the dining room table, where I carefully opened the box to find a dozen of the most beautiful red roses I had ever seen. My swollen nose stuck down into the middle of a rose in search of its scent, I began to fumble for the envelope that had accompanied the flowers. I pulled out the card with excitement as well as curiosity, for there was no occasion, no reason for me to be receiving flowers.

I read the words on the card.

"Happy Mother's Day," the card read simply. "May God bless you."

It was signed, "Love, Matt."

And Time Stood Still.

I leaned heavily against the table, taken aback by the name on the card.

Matt was not my husband. Matt was my brother. My beloved younger brother. Matt was Private First Class Cullers of the US Air Force, stationed far, far away in Seoul, South Korea. He was only twenty years old, and he had been in Korea for sixteen months.

Private First Class Cullers had stood in line for twelve hours for his turn to place a flower order, stood in line with all the other young soldiers who wished to send flowers and messages of love to their mothers and wives at home. The hours passed were nighttime hours, and there would be no opportunity to make up the lost sleep before the next day's demanding routine. They didn't mind. The young soldiers stood in line through the night, talking quietly, laughing at each other's jokes and telling stories of home to pass the time.

Cradling the card in my hand, I felt profoundly moved by my brother's act of Love. My brother, a soldier, was remembering me with tenderness and calling me mother when all the world still labeled me "expecting." As I looked at his name on the card, the feeling of love I felt for my brother began to expand until it became Something Else as well. Instinctively laying a hand over my heart, I trembled as I felt Love's presence…I felt God's presence.

Rereading the card, looking at the words "May God bless you," I felt the Blessing. It was as simple as that. I felt God's assurance, felt Something Loving telling me that I would be "just fine" as a mother, and that I would be blessed. And I have been.

When young soldiers lay aside the heavy burdens of the day in order to send messages of love and reassurance to mothers and sisters and wives at home, is this not God? And I ask you, if this isn't God, then…what is?

God is a Soldier, loving you.

Sighting Eleven
GOD WATCHES
CHESS TOURNAMENTS

Such is the power of love,
that it transforms the lover into the Beloved.

HUGH OF ST. VICTOR

THEY SCRAMBLED IN AT THE LAST MINUTE early that Saturday morning with tousled hair and crooked grins, eyes still puffy from sleep, some skipping breakfast to make it to the school on time, some walking from home to be there, some riding bikes, some lucky enough to catch a ride with a parent on their way to work. They skipped soccer games and football games, dance classes and music lessons to be there that day. They didn't care, not a bit. It was a small price to pay to participate in the Annual Spring Chess Tournament for the elementary school, third through sixth grade.

The boys and girls prepared for the tournament for almost

a year, meeting every Tuesday after school. Anyone was welcome in chess club. You didn't have to be smart, or popular, or anything special at all. You didn't even have to know how to play chess. Mr. A would teach you how to play the game, and the club members engaged you in matches to help you learn.

The tournament is an all-day, multiple-round event. This is carefully explained to the parents in the cafeteria before they are invited to stay, or leave, as they see fit. The teachers explain kindly that they understand that Saturday is a busy day for families, many of them with two working parents. They reassure the parents that it's okay if they can't stay—school employees have volunteered to watch over the children that day. Teachers, the school nurse, the secretaries, even the principal is present. The cafeteria serves an inexpensive lunch. The computer lab is open, as is the gym, so the children have something constructive to do between matches. It's a gift, pure and simple, from the school to the children.

Some parents, with a quick hug and a wish for good luck, left to run necessary errands or go to work. Others pulled out a thick book or an iPad to read, planning to stay for the day. As goodbyes and good lucks were exchanged between children and parents, the children who had walked, biked, or been dropped at the door moved restlessly about the gym, jostling one another and joking, enjoying the freedom of attending the event parent-free. One or two, however, stood awkwardly apart, silent, like the slight blond boy near the water fountain.

The young boy stood at the water fountain, alone, shoulder against the wall, head down. He fidgeted with a pencil self-consciously, pretending not to notice the commotion. But he stole a glance, from time to time, at the others in the gym, and then at the door, not hoping, really, just…looking. His lips pressed together, his suppressed sigh betrayed by the lift and fall of his chest, he lowered his head again and tapped his pencil against his palm. Tap-tap-tap. Tap-tap-tap. *It's-o-kay. It's-o-kay…*

• • • • •

I don't know how to play chess. But I stay to watch the tournaments anyway. I like watching the children. I like catching the flash of a dimple, a smothered laugh, a hand clapped over a mouth in the shape of an "O" when a player realizes she's just been checkmated, watching the winner and the loser leave together to go play in the gym "until next time," good-naturedly punching each other's shoulders. I feel as if I'm watching children at their very best, as if I'm watching Who They Really Are before the world convinces them otherwise.

• • • • •

On this tournament day, as the children filed quietly into the library and seated themselves across from each other at long lines of tables, there was a "fresh" feeling in the air. It wasn't just the crisp spring air flooding the room from the open windows, it was something that emanated from the children as well, as they grinned at each other from across the tables, waiting for the signal to begin. On this day, they were all the same. All would win, all would lose. They wished each other good luck as they shook hands like grown men and women.

Watching the children during the late morning match, I noticed an odor in the room that contrasted sharply with the fresh air I had been enjoying, an odor vaguely reminiscent of my garage, like sweat and dirt and gas and grease. Stretching my neck and rotating my shoulders, I began to look around idly. The seat next to me was empty; the mother seated there had left some time ago to join her child in the hallway at his match's end. As I looked about, I noticed that next to the vacant chair beside me sat a man I had not seen before. The man was huge, a muscular man, and his body seemed far too large for the little folding chair on which he sat. He had bushy black hair that flowed to his shoulders and a dark beard and mustache to match. He was a hulking figure, almost threatening. I immediately forgot about locating the source of the odor as I began to speculate about who the man was. Our community was small, and I was surprised that I did not recognize him. He hadn't been in the cafeteria that morning, nor at the beginning of this match, I was certain. I ran my gaze over the remaining children and began matching children to parents, trying by process of elimination to determine which child the man was present for. As I turned my perplexed gaze from the children back to the man's face, I was struck by his expression and I became instantly alert.

The fierce-looking man's face bore a profoundly tender expression as he watched a young boy at the first table…an expression that seemed strangely out of place under bushy black eyebrows and a deeply furrowed brow. I looked again from the man to the table he seemed to be watching, and I recognized the thin blond boy who had stood alone, restless and uncomfortable, next to the water fountain that morning. Him? He was here for the boy? I quickly returned my gaze to the man, who remained oblivious to my inspection, and I watched him as he watched the boy. His eyes never left the boy's face. My heart began to thud-thud-thud looking at that face, and Time Stood Still.

I looked back at the boy just in time to see the boy look up and see the man. The boy's eyes lit up at the sight of the man and he smiled. It was radiant like the sun, that smile, a smile of pure joy, and the boy's face became animated. The man smiled in return, slow and easy under the bushy mustache, the light in the boy's eyes reflected in his own, and he nodded slowly, just once. The boy straightened in his chair and returned to his match, his body no longer awkward and strained but now fluid and energetic.

As I watched the man watch only the boy's face, never his moves on the board, it occurred to me that the man did not know how to play the game—just like me. It was then that I noticed his hands, resting on sturdy knees, large fingers spread apart. They were dirty. There was black grime caked under his fingernails. In fact, I noted for the first time, his clothes were dirty as well.

The odor, I realized, was coming from *him*.

I shifted in my chair to look at the man more closely. His dirty clothing was a work uniform. I glanced at the clock, and suddenly all the pieces fell into place. The man had to work today. Hard work. Dirty work. He took the only free time he had, lunchtime, to come and watch a boy play a game he himself did not know. Just to Be There. Just to Love him.

The boy was looking at the man again, smiling; and the man's face was filled with love and encouragement. I looked down and blinked back tears. I realized that I was sitting but one seat away from God.

God watches chess tournaments.

Even if He has to skip lunch.

Sighting Twelve
GOD SINGS

God sent his Singers upon earth
With songs of sadness and of mirth,
That they might touch the hearts of men,
And bring them back to heaven again.

HENRY WADSWORTH LONGFELLOW
"THE SINGERS"

SHE WAS RAISED BY PARENTS WHO BELIEVE. Which was incredibly uncomfortable for her because she never quite could. She wanted to believe, but none of it—none of those things her parents believed in—seemed very likely. She was very smart (gifted, the teachers said), and her sharp, rational mind could make no sense of any of it.

In eighth grade, she told her parents she did not want to be confirmed into the Catholic faith. She didn't want to confirm long-ago baptismal promises made on her behalf...because she didn't believe. But they made her. Her parents *made* her get confirmed. She stood with her classmates and confirmed a set of statements she did not believe in, because her parents would take away her social media privileges if she didn't. And Grandma and Grandpa, whom the girl loved dearly, would be disappointed if she refused.

She was glad to grow up, become her own woman and leave it all behind. So. Glad.

And yet…

She isn't just smart. She has a beautiful voice that is classically trained. So on Sundays you will find her singing for the Unitarians as they sing along and clap their hands—because they pay her. Or she is making the Catholic mothers cry as she sings the "Ave Maria"—because they pay her. Or she is delighting the Episcopalians with a solo, which she does, she will tell you…because they pay.

"It's a gig," she says matter-of-factly. "I make to-do lists in my head while I wait to sing." To make sure you understand that she is not a believer, she pushes again, looking at you sharply, adding, "On one of my jobs I was in the choir loft, and I checked text messages during the sermon."

But if you swallow your discomfort and listen, she says other things, too. The Episcopalian priest, his sermons are practical, and she respects that. The Methodists are *SO* intense about outreach that they make her a little uncomfortable, but she thinks they mean well, and CAN YOU BELIEVE the Catholics changed some of the words of the service? ("It's more flowery now," she says, shrugging. "I don't like it.")

When you hear her sing, you would never guess…

You would never guess she does not BELIEVE. She's beautiful in a breathtaking, clean, holy kind of way. Eyes framed by impossibly long, thick black lashes. Eyes that glow like dark coals against flawless porcelain skin. And when she lifts those eyes up to the heavens, you can see the dazzling darkness of those eyes.

You see, too, the lift of a feathery brow, the tilt of a petite chin, the in and out flash of a dimple. And when the perfectly shaped pink lips move and take shape to allow The Sound to escape, you think…

You think…

You think an angel is singing, not a nonbeliever.

Of course, *I* know this because *I've* heard her sing.

• • • • •

I was sitting in a church one sunny Sunday morning, sunlight streaming in through stained-glass windows, when a dark-haired, dark-eyed beauty moved from her place in the choir to stand before a microphone placed near the center of the altar.

There was a sense of Stillness about her as she stood there, quiet, composed, poised. The pianist struck a single note. Only one. Then she slowly removed her hands from the keyboard and folded them in her lap. The pianist lifted her eyes, looked at the girl, and then gracefully inclined her head. The girl took a deep breath, opened her mouth…and the sound that came out was so full of strength and power and beauty that I was stunned. I literally gasped.

The Sound quickly filled the room, soaring and diving then soaring again. I could feel it vibrating through the church, vibrating through *me*. The Sound seemed to grab my Soul, intensify it, expand it, magnify it, until my Soul and The Sound became all mixed together and I felt…exalted.

Looking up at the altar, I began to cry. I wept because of the beautiful sound she made, and I wept because when I looked up at the altar, God was there. He was there. Singing with her. Through her. As her. And God looked so…happy.

As they sang together, God and the girl, it crept over me slowly—God loves the beautiful nonbeliever very much. And even though He respects her freewill choice to See-Him-Not, He longs to have her visit His house sometimes. So He gives her money.

Come sing for My people, He says. *I'll pay you.*

So the beautiful nonbeliever comes into His houses every week and sings for money. And when she sings, God sings with her.

Sighting Thirteen
GOD PAINTS NAILS

Flowers are love's truest language.

PARK BENJAMIN

THE TOWN WAS GROWING, that was certain. *To think* that now the ladies did not have to leave town and drive to a bigger city nearby to get their nails done. Oh, yes, the town was definitely growing.

The two women were abuzz with stories of growth and stories of gossip as they sat on the leather couch in the new nail salon waiting their turns. Growth was good, they agreed, but not *too* much growth. The nail salon was good, Walmart was bad. Walmart would put the local businessmen and women out of business, and the traffic—good heavens!—it would be awful. Just like it was for the annual Pork Festival when people drove in from all over the county to celebrate the wonder of pork at the local fairgrounds.

The ladies agreed that it would be best if the town council voted the Walmart proposal down, and the woman with the large diamond on her finger bobbed her head smartly and remarked with a knowing tone and a lift of the eyebrow that she would make sure she "had a word" with one or two of the council members…good friends of hers, after all. Her companion, eyes wide and admiring, nodded respectfully.

The nail salon, however, was good. Another small business, one that did not threaten any of the old-timers, and one that made things so *convenient*. And the new owners were so very service oriented. But *of course*, the woman with the diamond continued on, everyone knew about the Vietnamese and their work ethic. So refreshing in this day and age. And the solution they used for the fake nails—*fabulous*. Why rumor had it—and here the ladies moved closer together, voices dropping to a conspiratorial tone— that whatever they were using, well, it was *practically illegal*, whatever it was, but it was strong and the nails never broke. Most likely, the owners *knew* people, you know, people *like them*, who could get a hold of these kinds of things. They have their ways, you know. The women paused then to beam at the young Vietnamese owner and his charming little wife, and if the smiles were patronizing, the young man and woman pretended not to notice.

Yes, this was very good indeed, the woman with the large diamond remarked with a final decisive nod of her head. But don't—don't—let *him* do your nails. She raised the hand with the diamond to point, with no attempt to hide the motion, to an older gentleman who was working quietly on a woman's hands. *He* did her nails last time, and they were *horrible*. She told him JUST how she liked them done, and he *still* cut her nails too short. Well. Never again. When she signed in today, she requested the owner by name. And when he worked on her nails, why, she was going to let him know how disappointed she was last time. They needed to know, after all. Bad for business, a man like that.

Her passive listener nodded, expression attentive, head bobbing, as she murmured her assent, pretending to look as confident and knowing as her friend.

Yes, oh, yes. Bad for business indeed.

· · · · ·

The old man who was the topic of discussion finished with his customer, and after thanking her in his soft melodic voice, moved smoothly to the front of the salon to check the sign-in sheet at the front desk for the next name. As he struggled to pronounce the name on the list, the woman with the diamond interrupted curtly. "No. That's me. I'm waiting for Lee." The old man bowed to her courteously and called the next name on the list. Receiving a warning glance from Diamond Finger, the woman stammered awkwardly, "Um. Yes. Well…I'm…waiting for Mai." The old man merely inclined his head respectfully.

Oh god. That leaves me, I thought with dismay. I had heard every word of the ladies' conversation, even when they pretended to lower their voices. Panicked, I considered claiming that I was waiting for Lee as well, but as the old man attempted to pronounce my name, his voice so quiet I could barely hear him, "Caw-lee?" I couldn't do it. My heart sank and I stood up and forced a smile. I was not confident and assertive like Diamond Finger, and I was afraid of hurting the man's feelings.

As I followed the gentleman to his table, the derisive little voice in my head crowed its delight. *Oh that's just great. That's so you. Never have the guts to speak up. Now you're gonna spend money you don't have on one of the few things you do for yourself and he's gonna ruin your nails. And you, you won't say a word. You'll hate it, but you won't say a word.*

I took my seat reluctantly.

It's not even, the voice continued slyly, *that you're doing this to be kind to him. You just plain old don't have the guts to speak up.*

The voice was right. I didn't feel kind and I didn't feel full of compassion and love. I felt angry and resentful at the position the women had placed me in. And the voice was right, I was just a coward.

The voice continued, *People like you—*

The sound of the voice was unexpectedly interrupted by another voice. I was almost certain I had heard the word "flowers."

I came to with a start and looked apologetically at the old man. "I'm sorry." I stammered. "I was…er…daydreaming. Did you say something about flowers?"

He smiled and bobbed his head, and I noticed that despite the gray hair, he had very beautiful dark eyes behind the glasses he wore. His eyes were almost black. He smiled again, timidly, revealing teeth that were slightly crooked but very white.

"I say, it has been good spring for flowers."

"Oh, my, yes! It has, hasn't it?" I responded, the voice in my head temporarily forgotten and my enthusiasm sincere. "Do you know much about flowers?" I asked eagerly.

I was, for the first time in my life, trying to learn about flowers. I wanted beautiful flower beds like the ones I admired in the magazines, beautiful, full, unstructured flower beds with all different types of flowers spilling into one another. But I'd never grown flowers, I did not have the instinctive knack of a "natural," and everything I planted died. Reading about gardening was overwhelming for me. Apparently I needed to know about soil type and fertilizers, zones and degrees of hardiness, how to water enough but not too much. I would inevitably close the book with a sigh and search my mind—surely there was *someone* I knew who could just help me along a little, tell me what to do, explain it so it made sense.

"A little."

"Oh. Well. I'm just a beginner," I sighed. "I keep killing things. What do you have?"

The old man smiled shyly, and as he returned to his work on my hands, he began to talk to me, speaking quietly and slowly, about the flowers he grew, where he placed them so that they would thrive, how often he watered them and when.

I listened closely, taking mental notes as best I could. I forgot my nails and the mean little voice as I sedulously gathered information.

We were interrupted by the owner, who had left his chair across from Diamond Finger to come and stand over the old man. He spoke rapidly in his native tongue, and his wife came to join him. Standing over the man, they continued, speaking with each other and to the man as well, the sounds of their language sounding sharp and staccato to my ears. There was motioning toward my hands, and the husband and wife seemed to be discussing something. I threw a glance at Diamond Finger, who was watching us keenly. Has she spoken to the owner already? I wondered. Complained about the old man?

I felt strangely defensive of the gentle man working on my nails. *Oh, how embarrassing for him that they should do this to him here, now!* I thought. Suddenly, I wanted to help the old man. I mustered all the spunk I could find within myself, straightened my shoulders, tipped my chin and pretended that *I* was a Somebody, just like Diamond Finger. Looking directly at the owner and his wife, I lifted an eyebrow—just like Diamond Finger had—and widened my eyes as if to say, "Why, whatever could be the matter?" I did my very best to convey through my expression that I was perfectly happy with the work being done on my hands, and that I couldn't imagine why they would be intruding. They returned to their chairs, continuing to discuss the matter in abrupt bursts of disjointed syllables punctuated with gesticulating hands. The old man continued to work, never looking up.

"I like them best in morning," he said quietly.

I was confused for a moment, my thoughts still focused on trying to determine whether or not the exchange had been about the old man. I speculated about the expression I had seen on Diamond Finger's face—watching us closely at first, lips pursed, then suddenly a puckering of her brow, her mouth opening just slightly, as if she breathed an "ooooohhh," then dropping her eyes and pretending to inspect her nails. She moved restlessly in her chair, as if she were uncomfortable.

I quickly realized that the old man was still talking about his flowers.

"The morning?" I asked.

"Yes. Morning. When no one else is up. It good time then." He looked up at me and smiled. "My son and his wife, they like to—how you say?—sleep in. 'Why you get up so early, Father?' they ask me. 'Sleep! Sleep in!'"

He laughed softly. "I do not understand this sleep in. I cannot sleep in. Morning is best time."

Morning is best time. I thought of my morning walks; and looking down at my hand, held by his as he worked, it slowly came over me that it was God who was holding my hand, teaching me about flowers and sharing with me His delight in the quiet morning hours of our world.

"Ohhhhh," I breathed in recognition. And then I said quietly, but intently, "You are right. Mornings are the best time."

He looked up and smiled again, and this time his smile was not shy but instead wide and sure. There was a strange light in the man's eyes.

Wow, I thought. *God!*

We talked a while longer, and then he was done. I thanked him for his flower advice and he, head bobbing up and down, thanked me for my tip. As I passed Diamond Finger and the owner, I hesitated.

"He did a great job!" I announced, looking the owner straight in the eye as I held up my fingers and wiggled them. "I am *very pleased*." I sounded confident and knowing, just like Diamond Finger. I turned to look triumphantly at Diamond Finger—after all, it was God I was defending and I felt strong—but where I expected to find indignant affront, I instead found relief in her eyes and on her face. I suddenly knew that the expression on her face before *had* been regret, after all, for causing the old man trouble.

I paused, freshly manicured hand resting against the door, to look back at God one last time. He raised His hand in a goodbye, then graced me with one last courteous bow of His head. And I knew, looking at Him like that, that God didn't need my defense. God, with His mornings and His flowers was doing *just fine*. The nails…why that's just something He does on the side in order to talk with His children.

Sighting Fourteen
GOD IS AN OLD WOMAN

He will wipe every tear from their eyes. There
will be no more death or mourning or crying or
pain, for the old order of things has passed away.

REVELATION 21:4

I NEVER KNEW WHY I LOVED HIM SO MUCH. I never asked myself why. I just *did*. As a teenager, sometimes I would have nightmares that he had died, and I would awaken, heart pounding, gasping for air and then—realizing it was only a dream—I would try to calm the terror I felt at the thought of a world without him in it. I would be haunted the next three or four days, haunted by fears that the dream was a premonition, not a nightmare. Haunted by thoughts of losing him.

For as long as I can remember, I loved him *specially*, a special love over and above the other loves that flowed through my life. And *he*—oh my heart—he loved me too.

• • • • •

Aprils are tricky in Ohio. They can be very rainy and very cold. Most years, you sigh and long for May, but sometimes, some sad times, you can't think of anything more appropriate than rain and cold in April. It is so appropriate, in fact, that anything else would be an affront.

I once stood in an Ohio cemetery in an April just like that. Five months pregnant with twins, I stood alone in the pouring rain, in the bone-chilling cold, crying helplessly and hopelessly before the freshly dug grave of my brother. We had buried him six weeks before.

My brother's love for me was unlike any love I had ever known. Unconditional. Unfailing. Always a ready smile, a welcome, an assurance that there was time—always time—for me. Understanding before I could finish but letting me finish anyway; empathizing with my fears before laughing them away; championing my every cause. For me, it was love without fear. He would always love me and he would always see the best in me, even when I couldn't see it myself. It's a miracle, that kind of love, but I lived every day so secure in it that I seldom gave the wonder of it any thought. Like my brother, the miracle was just…present.

Standing there, on that cold gray day, I was sick, sick, sick at heart; and the pain was beginning to feel like more than I could bear. As I stood there sobbing, I felt frozen in time. It would never stop raining…it would never stop hurting…and he would never come back. My thoughts became increasingly disordered, and I felt as if I were dying there too. I felt as if I *wanted* to die there. There was a sudden pressure in my chest, and I began to gasp for air.

There was movement in my peripheral vision, and I glanced to my right to see an elderly woman a short distance away. The small cemetery had been utterly empty when I arrived, and I had not seen a car enter, but I was too agonized to think anything at all about the woman's unexpected appearance. In fact, she seemed almost surreal. She was a blot of white, with her snowy white hair and her white woolen jacket. She was approaching me. I didn't care. I could only feel the pain and the unbearable pressure in my chest. *My brother!* My head began to spin, and there was a ringing in my ears as the grayest of days began to go black…

Another moment, and she was beside me, slipping an arm around my waist. "There, there, now, honey," she said. "It will be all right."

In the last six weeks, I had passionately hated anyone who suggested to me that it would "be all right." Because I knew that it was *not* going to be all right—ever again. But there was something different about the old woman. I felt a stillness about her, a quiet.

Collapsing against her, a hand to my throbbing head, my eyes fell upon a cross hanging around her neck, and I thought to myself, from some far-off place, how strange it was that the cross seemed to catch light and shine, even though there was no sun on this grayest of days.

Gently she stated, "You have lost someone."

"It's…my…brother," I choked out between sobs, and the heaviness was upon me again.

"Yes," she answered simply.

And suddenly I was telling her everything. Telling a total stranger everything I could not tell the others. Not the technicalities of the accident, which I could now recite by rote almost emotionlessly, but how much I loved him, how much it hurt, how I didn't know if I could live in this world without his presence. My words spilled out over each other until eventually, after a long, long while, there was simply nothing left to say.

It was still raining, and we were standing there unprotected, but I was not aware of being wet or cold. We stood in silence, except for the soft sound of the falling rain. I heard a train whistle blow in the distance, lone and mournful. And still we stood, she and I, looking down at my brother's headstone. After a long while, she spoke.

"It will be all right," she said. "I know it doesn't seem like it right now, but it will get better." Again, the faint note of authority. And with her words, inexplicably, a calm began to creep over me. The pain was still there, thudding dully with every beat of my heart, but it was no longer consuming me.

We stood quietly awhile longer. She did not ask if I was feeling better. She did not suggest that I return to my minivan. She did not ask if I'd be okay to drive, or if they'd be worried about me at home. She simply stood with me as if we had time...all the time in the world.

Standing there, stealing a look at an old, wrinkle-lined face that seemed full of beauty and grace, I realized that the rain had finally stopped. The woman turned and looked thoughtfully at me for a moment, and then, grasping both my hands in hers, she looked directly into my eyes and said firmly, "It will start getting better. You will never forget. You will still love him. But it will begin to get better." She paused. She seemed to straighten, become taller. Her shoulders square, her head erect, her eyes still holding my own, she assumed a Strength, a Power, an Authority, as she said quietly but firmly, "And *you know* you will see him again."

With that, she turned and walked away.

I didn't even stammer out a thank-you. I simply watched her walk away. She climbed into a white Cadillac and the car drove away.

White, I thought. *How appropriate.*

Sighting Fifteen
GOD IS A NURSE

The capacity to give one's attention to a
sufferer is a very rare and difficult thing; it is
almost a miracle; it is a miracle.

SIMONE WEIL

THE HOSPITAL CHAPLAIN, A NUN, for they were a Catholic family, asked the parents if they would like to have last rites administered. The doctors had not been able to turn the tide after all. In fact, they could not even offer the parents an explanation for the series of bizarre complications that had placed their firstborn child at death's door after she gave birth to full-term twins. The parents had lost a son six months before, and the mother sobbed brokenly to think that God could ask her for another child.

They agreed to have the rites performed. When the daughter regained consciousness, only briefly, her father gently explained it all to her; and with a breaking heart, she whispered to her father that she agreed the rites should be performed, for she felt death was very near.

As she slipped back into the dark realms of the unconscious, the rhythm of the last rites sounding in her ears, the girl could think only of her babies, and the two little ones at home, and she pleaded, at the last, with the little strength left in her, *God, please, no. Please don't take me from my children.*

The next morning, mysteriously and suddenly, for reasons the doctors were never able to pinpoint, the girl began to stabilize. Her nurses contacted her OB/GYN quickly, for they knew the good doctor would want to know right away, and the specialists as well.

The hospital was abuzz about the doctor. The gentle man shocked everyone when he fought fiercely against hospital authorities as they began making preparations to send the girl's healthy babies home after the standard three-day stay. He sensed instinctively that his patient needed her babies near. In the end, he vowed to pay the hospital bill personally if insurance would not. Upon hearing the news of the girl's turn for the better, the gentle Jewish doctor slipped quietly into the hospital chapel to whisper a heartfelt thank-you that the little Catholic mother would live to hold her babies.

It was, he thought, a miracle.

• • • • •

I was to live, after all. But when I awoke, I was not the girl I had been before the birth of my babies and the unexpected battle for my life. There had been...*complications*. According to the doctors, areas of my brain had been damaged. Whether the damage was permanent or temporary, no one could be sure. Since there was "no case on the books" like mine, the doctors would say with a helpless shrug of their shoulders, they simply could not tell us what to expect in the way of recovery—or whether full recovery could be expected at all.

One of the areas of damage involved the part of the brain that processes speech; my speech was impaired, much like a stroke victim. My heart ached for my two children at home—we had never been apart!—and for my babies, who were far away in another part of the hospital. Struggling to communicate, I would beg to see my babies, to go home to my children, and I would share my family's barely concealed horror at the sound of the incoherent sounds and syllables that came out of my mouth. I knew what I wanted to say; I just couldn't seem to say it. I would cry helplessly as the nurses and doctors patted my arm and told me that I needed to Focus on Getting Better. The physical pain in my head and throughout my body was a small matter compared to the heartache I felt at the separation from my children and my very Self. I was deeply frightened. There was fear all through me, fear and pain, and incredible, overwhelming sorrow and longing.

Until the day The Nurse walked in.

Her straight blond hair was caught in a neat ponytail that lay obediently down the center of her shoulder blades, and as she moved briskly about the room, I fancied I could hear the air crackle about her. I felt a Shift in the room when she walked in, and I thought the room seemed lighter somehow. I had seen my fair share of nurses, but when this Nurse walked in I became instantly alert, and I felt instinctively that it was good that she was there. The tight, frightened part of me relaxed, just a little. As she moved around the room in her competent, efficient manner, I felt myself relax, relax, relax. Something Reassuring moved through me, and for the first time since delivering the babies, I felt...*safe*. I continued to watch her move about the room, but I did not try to speak to her for fear that my words would come out as gibberish.

Then she was at my bedside. She bent over me, and the movement was swift and sure. "Let me see your tongue," she commanded.

What had she said? Discomfited, I could only stare at her dumbly, and she was forced to repeat her command—still firm, but speaking kindly this time.

"Let me see your tongue."

I slowly opened my mouth and painfully obeyed. I had terrible pain in my mouth, but to my befuddled mind it just seemed to be part of the overwhelming pain in my head, just another complication.

The Nurse exhaled sharply. "*Just* as I thought! We're going to *do* something about this."

I stared at her in confusion as she turned on her heel and moved toward the door to exit the room. I felt panicked. It felt as if Something Good was leaving the room. And as Something Good moved away, fear and anxiety returned to resume their places.

As she left, she was shaking her head, and I heard her remark quietly to herself something about "how they could have missed this."

Missed what? I wondered dully.

The Nurse returned a short time later, and again I felt that inexplicable lifting of my anxiety. Laying a smooth, delicately formed hand on my arm, she said gently, and slowly, so I could understand, "Honey, your tongue is swollen to three times its normal size. You chewed it up horribly during your seizures. I have something here that is going to make you feel much, much better."

The Nurse had chased down the doctor tending to rounds that morning and demanded a medicated mouthwash for my mangled mouth. She commanded me to open my mouth and swish the medicine around, and I complied. The liquid was cool, and the medicine in the fluid numbed my mouth pain almost instantly. She laughed softly as she watched my eyes widen with surprise and wonder.

"Three times a day, dear," she said. "Three times a day. Now spit."

Again, I complied. As she bustled about the room, a sense of calm began to permeate my mind and spirit. It seemed connected to The Nurse. I began to dread the moment she would leave the room. I felt certain she would take the calm with her. She shot me a smile before she left, and I—afraid to try to speak—lifted my hand in a wave instead, hoping my crooked smile conveyed my thanks.

Three times a day indeed. The medication dramatically decreased the swelling of my tongue. The cuts where I had bitten myself began to heal. Encouraged by the pain relief, I attempted to speak more often. To everyone's surprise and delight, slowly my words began to come out correctly. It was a miracle, the family murmured amongst themselves, once again. A miracle. The Nurse's medication should only have healed my tongue, but in some inexplicable way, on that day, the damaged sections of my brain began to heal as well.

I couldn't wait to see The Nurse again. Not just to thank her, but also because I wanted to FEEL the FEELING I felt when she was nearby. Every day I awoke and thought, *Today, surely!* I watched the door hopefully, but the days passed, and still she did not return.

Early one morning, two young LPNs came tumbling into my room, one full-figured and boisterous, black dreadlocks pulled into a fat ponytail, and the other thin and giggly, her short, fine brown hair held in place with a wide blue headband.

"YOU are getting your hair washed today," the boisterous girl announced. "It's been WAY TOO LONG. Girl, you gettin' NAPPY." This was accompanied by a smothered laugh from her helper.

I was embarrassed. I *was* getting better, but not better enough to think about things like my hair. It hadn't occurred to me that my hair had not been washed for two weeks. I stirred in the bed, attempted to sit up, and the nurse with the dreadlocks, who seemed to be in charge, laid a firm hand on me.

"Oh, no, honey," she said. "You have to stay in the bed. Don't worry, though. We'll still get your hair clean."

The slight girl with the headband promptly stuffed cotton balls in my ears while the boisterous one tore a plastic bag at the seam and proceeded to tie it on my head like a bandana.

"Don't worry. I won't tie it over your face," she joked, flashing me a smile, her partner giggling. "Just your head. The bag will catch the water."

They lifted my head gently, wrapped a towel around my neck and proceeded to wash my hair, their cheerful chatter sometimes punctuated with laughter.

"We're doing this *twice*," the boisterous one informed me bluntly. "You need it."

As her strong fingers worked their way over and over my scalp, and the good-natured laughter reached me through the cotton balls, my embarrassment dissipated. You aren't touched much in the neuroscience ward...not in soothing ways anyway. As she rinsed and rinsed my hair with her firm but careful hands, I peeked up at her face and suddenly thought of The Nurse who had not yet returned. It occurred to me in a flash that if anyone could tell me who The Nurse was, it would be this young LPN.

When we were done, I told my little story and asked about The Nurse.

I watched her face carefully.

"Well, I don't know, honey," she answered slowly, head cocked to the side, dreadlocks slipping onto her shoulder. "I just don't know who that would BE. And I've been here a year. Can you tell me what day or what shift?"

I was ready with "in the morning" and "maybe a Thursday."

She sighed. "No, honey. I really don't know who it was. It doesn't sound like anyone who works this floor regular. Maybe she was a temp." Seeing my dismay, she patted my arm encouragingly. "Who knows. Maybe she'll be back."

My stomach sinking, I swallowed my disappointment and thanked them for my clean hair. They gathered up their supplies and slipped out of the room.

I waited and waited for The Nurse, hoping she would return. I wanted to thank her for the medicine, and well, *everything*. I wanted to tell her that I knew Who She Was.

She never returned, but I have thanked Her, all the same. God is a Nurse, moving in and out of the rooms of the suffering.

Sighting Sixteen

GOD IS A TEENAGER

Beauty is not in the face;
beauty is a light in the heart.

KHALIL GIBRAN

WE LIVE IN A WORLD that celebrates the beautiful. We never have to ask ourselves what constitutes "beautiful," for we are surrounded by a plethora of media specifically designed to save us unnecessary wondering, designed to make sure that we never need to trouble ourselves with determining what is beautiful. Constantly, unceasingly, relentlessly we are told, with pictures, with words, with music videos and movies and magazines and so many, many advertisements.

It's hard living in a world that celebrates and rewards the beautiful if you're Not Beautiful. As a teenager, I railed against a world that would reward people solely for their appearance. It's what's *inside* that counts, I was sure of it. I vowed things would be different when I got older, and I looked forward to the day that I could help change how the world viewed *beautiful*.

But then I grew into adulthood, and I found that the system that operates to reward the beautiful is insidious, invasive, and *present* in every aspect of our society and our personal lives. I began to feel that if *I* wanted admiration, rewards, and success, then I better find a way to be beautiful too. The teenager within cried out her protest, but with a sorrowful shake of the head, I slowly turned my back to her.

I didn't have the money (or the courage) to hire a surgeon to augment my breasts and liposuction my thighs. So I googled free workouts and exercised at home. I ate less food and drank more water. I squeezed money out of the grocery fund for better-quality cosmetics and the latest anti-aging creams.

"I'm doing this for *me*," I claimed defiantly to family and friends, shoulders squared and chin tipped upward. And I closed my ears to the teenager who lived within me still, the teenager who asked me, simply, *Are you?*

I pushed hard, but it was never enough, of course. Never. Enough.

And then one day it became pointless…meaningless…and just too damn hard. No matter how hard I tried, I was not going to be the kind of beautiful the world celebrates. And I was just… tired of it all.

And the teenager within stood there still.

• • • • •

I stood in the checkout lane that day, utterly not beautiful. I'd thrown on a pair of black pants to cover the extra pounds, my hair was washed but not styled, instead pulled severely into a clip at the nape of my neck, and my face was scrubbed clean but bore not a speck—not a speck—of makeup. I'd been out of my expensive moisturizer for several weeks, and I had quickly rubbed *hand lotion* on my face that morning—not to fight aging, but simply because my skin felt dry and tight after I washed it and the hand lotion was, you know, *there.*

I didn't care. I just didn't. Life was hard and life was busy, and after all, what was the point? It was never going to happen. I was never going to be beautiful. I gazed dully at the magazines on either side of me in the checkout lane, magazines designed to help me be beautiful. "Be Naturally Slim and Never Diet Again," they cried. "Best Abs Ever!" "Age-Proof Your Body in 8 Steps"; "Lip Tips Make Yours Fuller, Smoother, Younger"; "Butt and Thigh Makeover!" And *People* magazine, if I cared to take the time to look within its cover, was pleased to reveal to me which of the Famous Beautiful People were beginning to sag.

I knew what the magazines would say about *me*. The magazines would say that sudden disregard for one's physical appearance was a sign of depression. They'd recommend I see a doctor and ask for medication…medication that would make me want to be beautiful again.

I felt the faintest stir of rebellion. *I don't think so.*

With a sigh I handed the cashier my Kroger card, barely glancing at her face. But as my glance fell to her name card, I paused. SUSHAW, it said. Not Susan, or Sue or Susie. SUSHAW. Something stirred again. I returned my gaze to her face and smiled in spite of myself. So young and so hip! Her short blond hair was thick, and it stuck out at the most interesting angles—and it did so effortlessly, with no evidence of gel or glue or wax or hairspray. Her bangs fell to just past her eyebrows, the sexiest place for bangs to fall, my hairdresser used to tell me. Her eyes were emerald green, truly green, not accentuated by colored contact lens. The hemp choker at her neck was not too high and not too low, just like the low-slung waist of her jeans. Her Kroger shirt just skimmed the top of the jeans, and on *her* the shirt did not look like a uniform requirement, but rather a shirt she threw on to match the choker. Her nails were short and well manicured, and they were her own. The smile she flashed me revealed straight white teeth between clear-glossed lips. Still…

I glanced back at the blond, bikini-clad model on the front of *Glamour* magazine, and then returned my gaze to Sushaw. *Not beautiful,* I caught myself thinking, *but...* I stopped there, unable to finish my own thought. But what? Stealing another look at Sushaw, I suddenly realized that I couldn't think of any better way, any more interesting way for Sushaw to look. My thoughts, suddenly unblocked, continued in a rush. *Amazing...perfect...why yes, beautiful! In a most extraordinary way!*

Sushaw looked up at me just then to announce my total and caught me staring at her. I smiled a quick smile, embarrassed, and began digging in my purse for my debit card.

"You have a cute smile."

Assuming Sushaw was speaking to my son, I stopped digging to look up and enjoy the moment. I'd look up, and she'd be smiling at my son and he'd be grinning at her, the kind of moment young mothers love. Only...Sushaw wasn't looking at my son. I almost dropped my purse when I raised my eyes to discover that Sushaw was looking at, and speaking to, *me.*

I was suddenly acutely aware of my appearance. The pants, the pounds, the hair, the makeupless face. How dull I must look! How could this girl, this hip young girl, possibly be remarking on my smile?

But she was.

Now painfully self-conscious, I could only stammer my thanks. "Oh my goodness! Me? Thank you."

Flustered, I returned to my purse, blurting, "I guess you've made my day. I don't get many compliments."

There was a slight pause.

"Oh. Really. Why not?"

I stopped digging again to raise my glance, sharply this time, to Sushaw's face. *Oh, God, I was right,* I thought. *The girl feels sorry for me! I look so bad that she's trying to cheer me up.*

But Sushaw's expression was absolutely devoid of artifice or pity. The emerald green eyes were quiet, expectant, and met mine straight on. And as I looked into her eyes, Time Stood Still. The teenager within stepped forward, after all those heartsick years, to gaze with wonder into the eyes of God.

Why not?

"Well, hmm. I'm not sure," I said finally, breaking the spell. Then I laughed, light and free, like the teenager within. "Why not?" I said, turning to tease my son, poking him playfully in the shoulder. "Why shouldn't I get compliments?"

I picked up my bags and I smiled gratefully at Sushaw. "Thank you."

"Sure," Sushaw said. "Have a good day."

I saw Sushaw only once after that day. I was in the lane next to hers, two carts back, and I saw a flash of her shoes—a pair of old black-and-white Converse sneakers. The white canvas covering the toes had been written on with black marker. *What did it say?*

I stepped over and pretended to check the contents of the cooler placed between the two aisles, leaning slightly to the left to steal a look at her shoes. I was curious to see what a girl like Sushaw would write on her Converse tennis shoes. Despite my best efforts I caught only a glimpse, but I will always remember the word I saw:

Jesus.

Sighting Seventeen
GOD GOES TO FESTIVALS

The nation of Love differs from all others,
Lovers bear allegiance to no nation or sect.

MEVLANA JALALU'DDIN RUMI

IN THIS BIG, NOISY, CLAMORING NATION there are little places, tucked away here and there, surrounded by "nothing important." You cannot call these places secret; no one attempts to conceal them from knowledge or view. You cannot call them forgotten, because those who Know never forget. They are simply… overlooked. And therein lies their magic. Absent the interference and the demands of the big and the loud, the members of these communities are free to do as they please; and they are not just marching to the beat of their own drums—they are dancing.

In these little places, parents send their children to the same school they attended long ago, and the grandparents too; and they send them with the children of their own long-ago classmates. The local mechanic who does body work on everyone's cars is known to be a kind and generous man. He works long hours in the garage alongside his employees, and he misses his wife very much. He helps every year with the local 4-H club. The committee head of the PTA Fall Carnival worked for a traveling circus in the long-ago days before she went back to school for a master's degree in education, and her friends from those circus days still show up with carloads of prizes for the carnival every year. She's Director of Religious Education for the elementary school children at the little Catholic church now, and though her health binds her to a wheelchair, she works tirelessly for the children anyway. When her large frame rolls down the church aisle in her electric wheelchair, the children look at her with love and the adults look at her with respect.

In these small places, a teacher can hang a cross outside his classroom door with the words "He is Risen" at Easter time, and no one calls the principal to complain—even though it *is* a public school. The independent grocer can make a living here, although the bagboys' "tips" often consist of advice regarding the previous week's high school football win, and end with instructions to "tell your mother I said hello."

There are no Starbucks, but there are coffee shops with interesting names, high ceilings, live plants, and a small stage where remarkably gifted but as yet unknown musicians come to sing and play. You may see a sign above the door as you enter, a favorite of the owner, which announces, "You are now leaving the fast track."

There's a bank that bears the town's name, a courthouse that was built in the 1800s, and a running joke amongst the locals that the town has the same number of attorneys today as it did during the Civil War...it just never seemed to need any more. The children have Christmas parades that end in the center of town where they line up in rows on the steps of that magnificent old courthouse and sing Christmas carols, and everybody attends, drinking hot chocolate and stamping their feet to stay warm, speculating as to whether it was this cold last year.

In these little places, it's not just mainstream holidays that are celebrated. There are entire festivals for apples, strawberries, black walnuts...

Even *pork*.

• • • • •

And so it was, on Saturday, September 15, 2001, a mere four days after the terrorist attack on America, that I found myself attending the Great Preble County Pork Festival. With no one to tell them otherwise, the community leaders were free to decide that even though folks were greatly shaken and profoundly saddened by the previous days' events, it would be best to continue with the festival. It was a good time to be with family and friends, they reasoned, and it would be good for folks to laugh and sing and eat a little.

I was standing, as were others, listening intently to the music of *Americamanta*, an indigenous musical group from Otavalo-Ecuador. It was a mystery how the event organizers stumbled upon a group that at first blush would seem out of place in a small Midwestern community, but the first year the group appeared the folks had liked them very much, and the group was asked to return to the festival each year thereafter. Folks came to expect it.

The rhythm of the drums this day was soothing, the guitars captivating; but there was something almost mesmerizing about the sound of the native flutes and Andean pan-pipes. As the sound of the music floated out into the air, the huge, fresh, wide-open country air, I took a deep breath. Yet, just as I started to relax, the events of the week were upon me again, and the horror of it began to wash over me.

The events appeared in my mind as a series of flashes: <flash> The towers burning. <flash> The agonized faces. <flash> The stammering, stunned broadcasters. <flash> The grim reports. It was almost as if I could feel the people around me feeling it too. I could feel how shaken they were by the week's events, how wounded, how sore.

But I could also feel their gentleness with one another on This Day in the face of it all; and suddenly I felt it again, that mysterious thing I call The Shift.

God was here, I could feel it. Now, to find Him.

I began to scan the faces around me, searching for God. Mixed in with the flashes from the week gone by, other pictures began to present themselves to my searching eyes. <flash> The broad planes of the musicians' faces, the look in their large dark eyes as they seemed to communicate with each other without speaking. <flash> My little daughter quietly approaching the open guitar case, her small brown hands dropping in some of her hard-earned allowance to thank the musicians. <flash> The look on my son's face as he squinted in the sun and listened intently to the music...

Something inside of me seemed to expand as the flashes continued and became broader still. <flash> The man across the way in the wheelchair and the woman bent over murmuring in his ear, making him smile. The swaying teenage girls nearby with daisies painted on their cheeks. The gentle murmur of people speaking and laughing as they visited the nearby vendors. The blue, cloudless sky above us. The air and how fresh and cool it felt when I inhaled.

I felt myself begin to shake a little as I came to understand that it wasn't just God and me this time. This time, I found Him on every face. In fact, there was nowhere He was Not. Time Stood Still as I slowly came to understand, perhaps for the first time, that it wasn't just This Day…it was *every* day. Every day there is nowhere He is not.

Even that day. Even in those towers.

Sighting Eighteen
GOD VISITS THE SANTA SHOP

To be what we are, and to become what we are
capable of becoming, is the only end of life.

ROBERT LOUIS STEVENSON

"A PROFIT IS A GOOD THING, YES?" remarked one of the
board members, smiling affectionately at the Christmas chairwoman's obvious discomfort.

"Yes, but I wanted this to be for *the children*," she protested.

She had always been proud of the fact that she was good
with numbers. She had worked years as head legal secretary to
a prominent lawyer in a successful, big-city law firm before taking time off to be mother to the only child her body would ever
give her. "Let Jennie run the numbers," her boss would say back
then, and run them she would. She never made mistakes. Ever.
Now at home with her daughter, she kept the books for the local

church. Pastor Jim said she was a blessing and he didn't know what he'd do without her. Church members could ask questions about how money was being spent and she would know, right down to the penny. "It's a gift," the grand old ladies would tell her, their hats bobbing as they nodded their heads approvingly. They wouldn't worry a bit as long as Sister Jennie was a lookin' after the money.

Yet here she sat, trying to explain a profit that the book-work—*her* bookwork!—did not support. The PTA had recruited her as chairman of the Santa Shop because they thought she was smart, efficient, and competent. She sat there, cheeks flushed with embarrassment, shaking her head. What she didn't realize, as she turned her uncomfortable gaze upon the smiling board members, was that they had also recruited her because her heart was as kind as her mind was sharp.

It was her kind heart that moved her to suggest that the PTA not try to make a profit on the Santa Shop that year. It was for the children, after all, she urged. She was worried about the poorer families—their children would not have much money. "Let's find the best deal possible for the PTA," she pleaded, "and simply pass that on to the children. Let's sell them the items at cost."

The room remained quiet.

"I'm good with numbers," she rushed on. "I can make this work."

The board members agreed. She had their blessing and full support.

She researched their options thoroughly and exhaustively, struck the best deal possible for their little PTA, and then priced the items for the children's shop at cost. Yet here she sat, with a profit of several hundred dollars that she couldn't explain, a profit that she had specifically tried to prevent.

A few board members pretended to look over the figures at her insistence, but only to please her.

"Perhaps someone slipped money into the drawer?" one suggested with a yawn.

"No, indeed," she responded indignantly. She had overseen the operation of the cash registers *personally*. There were only two registers, and no one operated them except her and her assistant. And she had locked up the registers every time they were left unattended.

"Must be a God thing," remarked another one of the board members cheerfully with a smile and a dismissive shrug of her shoulders.

I leaned back in my chair and smiled. *Must be a God thing, indeed,* I thought.

It *was* a God thing, and I had good reason to know. *I* had seen God visit the Santa Shop on opening day and then return every day thereafter, as if He just couldn't resist dropping by. I saw all of it because I was the chairwoman's assistant, and I manned the second cash register.

• • • • •

The opening day of the Santa Shop is a grand day indeed. It's held on a Saturday morning so that Santa may visit the school, and the youngsters can have Breakfast with Santa. It's just donuts and juice, but it's free and the children think it's a great treat. After they eat, they sit on Santa's lap whispering the things that young believers always whisper, before racing off to their mothers to announce, "Mommy... He's the *real* Santa. I *know* it." They visit the shop with their parents, not to purchase anything—Mommy and Daddy might see!—but just to visit, and think, and plan for the week to come.

I was near the cafeteria door on opening day when a young toddler slipped while climbing up to the cafeteria table to eat his donut. He bumped his eye, and his upper brow immediately began to swell. While his mother carried him off to the nurse's station in search of ice, I offered to accompany his older brother and sister into the Santa Shop to pick out a toy to help distract their little brother from his discomfort. He liked cars, they told me, and fish. I watched them search for the perfect toy for their little brother. *They'll want something for themselves,* I thought. *It's understandable.*

I was wrong.

I watched the big sister reach past rings, necklaces, and body glitter to lay her hand upon the "perfect" truck. It was as if the other things weren't even there. I watched the brother overlook magnifying glasses, compasses, and yo-yos to reach a set of rubber fish. He never hesitated. They turned to me, eyes shining, just long enough to raise their choices up for my inspection; then they bounded from the room in search of their little brother without a backward glance. It was beautiful and it was pure. It was human nature at its very best.

Thinking of the children's selfless act, the light that shone in their eyes, their attitudes of joy, I thought impulsively, *This is Who We Really Are! This is who we came into the world to be.*

It would have been enough to witness that act and to see God shining back at me from the eyes of those children. But God must have enjoyed Himself very much that day, for He returned to the Santa Shop again and again the following week. And I, lucky girl, was there to see it all.

Sometimes a child visiting the shop would have no money. "Don't worry," I would hear God say. "I have some." And I'd look up to see God's chubby hand, full of money, reach out and place some of it into the slender hand that had none. Then off they'd go,

God and His friend, to giggle together and make their purchases.

Sometimes a child would want to buy something for himself, and he would have to make a decision between the gift he wanted for himself, and the gift he wanted to purchase for a family member. I'd look up to see God standing there, ready to assist, to suggest, to advise. I would listen to God carefully explain the child's options, and then tell the child very kindly, "This is up to you, though." I watched child after child place something they wanted for themselves back on a table in order to purchase a gift for a family member instead. God would lean down and say quietly, "Your mommy will love that necklace. But she will be especially happy when she knows that you chose a necklace for her even though you wanted that watch for yourself. Those things mean a lot to mommies, you know." The child would look up at God for a moment and then nod solemnly, and God would smile, and the child would smile, and it was as if Light flooded the entire room. An occasional child would choose to buy for herself instead of a family member. There was no reproach, no judgment. God would just smile and pat the child's head, as if to say, *Soon, child, soon.*

"I told David to pick something out for himself," a voice whispered into my ear one day. "It's a gift from me. Don't worry. My class will understand." I raised my eyes to see the speaker, and looking into God's face before me, I had no doubt that under Her careful guidance the class would not begrudge David his little gift, but rather, would *want* David to have a gift. David, who'd had so little joy and so much pain.

On another day, overhearing the chairwoman's remark that we were shorthanded for the afternoon, God volunteered to stay and help. Oh, no, the chairwoman protested, you've done enough just working with us this morning! God just smiled and said there wasn't much happening at the Senior Citizen Center that afternoon anyway, and that She'd like to stay and help with the children, if we didn't mind.

As the children struggled with their math skills, they occasionally discovered at the cash register that they were short fifty or seventy-five cents. Invariably, God would lean down to whisper in my ear, "Go ahead. I'll cover it." As the child turned away, God dropped the quarters in the drawer with a smile, and then off He'd go, humming under His breath.

The human faces that appeared to me over the course of that week changed, but the Divine One did not. *Oh, God*, I sighed, over and over that week. *It's true, it's true. This is Who We Really Are, isn't it?*

• • • • •

I thought of all these things as I sat in the meeting. It made me laugh, thinking about the profit. I thought how like God it was to leave money behind as well. Like the teenagers who scrawl graffiti on the local barns (*DJ was here!*), I could imagine God laughing, leaving money in the drawer in case we should ever doubt that He had dropped by.

I finally spoke up, throwing a reassuring smile in the direction of the beloved chairwoman. "She's right," I said, nodding toward the cheerful board member. "It's a God thing."

Sighting Nineteen
GOD EATS DORITOS

If help and salvation are to come,
they can come only from the children.
For the children are the makers of men.

MARIA MONTESSORI

SHE IS ONE OF THOSE CHILDREN you hear about but think it can't be true—one of those children who could die with even "a trace" ingestion of an allergen, one of those children who would react to even "contact exposure." She has a fatal allergy to peanuts, tree nuts, and all their byproducts, and the doctors don't know why. It's sad but simple. If she eats the wrong food, she will die. If the wrong food touches her skin, she will become ill.

She is my daughter.

When she was little, it was easy to keep her with me always, it was easy to keep her safe. But as she grew, she longed to join the world and all its wonders. To my dismay, her specialist agreed with her. I was not to keep her at home; I was to teach her how to live in the world.

It was a matter of great sorrow for me that I also had to teach my daughter why some of the grownups in her world grew angry at the sacrifices they were asked to make on her behalf. There is no easy way to tell a child with a disability that the grownups don't think he or she is "worth" the sacrifice. For her sake, I would tell her, with an exaggerated sigh, and a regretful shake of the head, that the grownups, well, they just didn't *understand*, but we would be patient, wouldn't we, and soon they *would* understand, and then they wouldn't mind so much that they couldn't send M&Ms and Reese's Cups into the classroom for party treats. She would nod her head solemnly to please me, brown curls bouncing, but looking into those serious eyes, my heart would begin to pound as I could see my failure reflected there, and that my child was in pain, knowing that some people thought she wasn't worth the sacrifice. Anxious for her safety, and worried about her tender heart, I was often sad, and I longed for the days when she was mine, only mine, living quietly in the big green house.

Everything changed one bright summer day at the pool.

• • • • •

The lifeguards had just blown their whistles for the scheduled rest break that was part of every hour of pool time. It was a quarter to noon, and mothers about the pool began to unpack lunches from brightly colored coolers prepared earlier that morning. My daughter scampered over to me with another little girl in tow. They stood in front of me giggling, wrapped in towels, hair dripping, while my daughter, in her best formal voice, "presented" her friend to me. I had barely smiled my hello to her new friend before my daughter interrupted me to ask if she could sit with her friend on her friend's blanket.

The familiar knot in my stomach returned, as I prepared to inquire what the friend would be eating. Was it peanut butter? If so, I would have to explain why they probably shouldn't sit together, and why her friend would have to wash her hands before playing with my daughter again. I would have to meet her mother and explain it to her as well. It was a wearying business, I confess, and I lived in dread of parents' reactions. Would they be understanding? Incredulous? Rude? Would my daughter be saddened by their reaction?

I took a deep breath and prepared to begin. But before I could say a word, the new friend moved closer to my daughter, their shoulders now touching.

"I'm not eating my sandwich," the new friend announced to me brightly.

"What?" I replied, confused by her announcement.

"I know all about Emma," she said airily. "My babysitter packed peanut butter today, and I told her not to even take it out of the bag. I don't want it. I want to sit with Emma." Looking up from my seat on the beach towel, squinting in the sun to better see her face, I looked up into a pair of eyes as blue as the cloudless sky behind her, eyes that were meeting my own with a serene, steady gaze, a gaze that seemed much older than the little face that surrounded it.

She was only a first-grader.

Swallowing the lump in my throat, I said gratefully, "Oh, sweetheart! That is so kind of you. But I can't let you skip your lunch! Emma can sit with me while you eat then wash your hands. I'll explain to your babysitter. You can play after rest break."

"Nope," she responded cheerily with a slight shake of her head. Dropping her towel in order to drape an arm around my daughter's shoulders, she remarked simply, "I want Emma."

I glanced at my daughter, and suddenly, Time Stood Still. The look on her face—it was radiant, like the sun. I could *feel* her joy, feel her rejoicing. She was *worth it*.

Touched by the girl's sacrifice and the profound effect it was having on my daughter, I stammered out falteringly, "Honey, your mother wouldn't want you to skip lunch."

"Oh, she won't mind," she countered confidently. She flashed me a grin. "Besides, we'll eat Doritos."

Absent her mother's permission, I knew I had no right to allow the girl to sacrifice her sandwich for a chips-only lunch, but I did it anyway. Maybe I shouldn't have. But I did. There was something about those clear, confident blue eyes…and the look of joy on my own daughter's face.

"Well…okay," I managed.

They squealed with delight at their success and ran off to plop down on the girl's blanket a short distance away. They waved at me gleefully. I was watching them, their little heads together, laughing and telling each other little girl things, sharing their chips, when the new friend looked up and smiled at me from across the way.

It was then, in that moment, that it struck me; and it ran through me like a jolt of electricity. I sat there, stunned. I could not believe what I was seeing.

It was God. Eating Doritos with my daughter. Sacrificing Her lunch, so that my daughter could "be" with Her. *Choosing* my daughter. Making her feel valuable and special…making her feel *worth it*. The girl smiled at me once more, as if She knew my thoughts, and then turned Her attention back to my daughter.

Everything changed that day. Everything. God started showing up everywhere to look after my daughter. Children announced to surprised parents that they didn't want to pack peanut butter and jelly for lunch—turkey was just as good anyway. Pulling out of the driveway for practice, soccer parents were instructed by their own children to turn back so they could run into the house to wash their hands—Emma was coming to practice! Parents sent Skittles and Starbursts to class parties instead of M&Ms and Reese's Cups. Kind-hearted mothers took it upon themselves to plan, unasked, nut-free birthday parties for their children so Emma could "laugh and play and not have to worry." Neighbors came to the door with labels for me to read. They wanted to give the neighborhood children a snack—was this one okay for Emma? When the nightly news featured a story about research for a vaccine, the phone rang and rang. Had we seen? Did we know? Could this help Emma?

God eats Doritos. And Everything changes.

Sighting Twenty
GOD IS A LITTLE BUDDHA

Most men are within a finger's breadth of
being mad.

DIOGENES THE CYNIC

THEY ARE GOOD AT SEEING THE BAD. They use their sharp minds to seek out the flaws, the pitfalls, the traps, the treacheries— in situations and in people. They are clever, clever at revealing all of life's ugliness to us. They know where to look and how to look, and they always operate from an understanding that there is no evil thing that man will not do to man. They should know. They've seen the evidence. They're our attorneys.

And we pay them to do this. We pay them well. We pay them to fight our enemies. We want our enemies exposed and punished. We want them punished for their betrayal, their neglect, their carelessness, for the wounds we've suffered at their most wicked hands.

We want our enemies punished *hard.*

We're certain that we stand in the right, and we're certain that with our attorney's help, this can be revealed. Should he suggest that perhaps we're not seeing clearly, we vehemently insist our position is sound. Should she suggest a compromise with our enemy, we are indignant. Should he suggest that a jury might not see things our way, we look at him askance and cry impatiently, "Well, what do you think *you're* for?"

We will not listen to carefully selected words of encouragement that point us in the direction of moving forward. Such suggestions are an affront to our sensibilities, and we make it clear that if he isn't willing to see things our way—and fight for it—then we'll take our money to someone who is.

Some Clever Ones convince themselves that they don't mind our demands. *It's only a game, after all,* they tell themselves and their peers, and they're good at it. They laugh as they smoke cigars and trade stories; they drive fast, expensive cars, drink lots of whiskey, and visit their vacation homes often. Should one of them ever have a moment, maybe two, when she feels a weariness, a regret, a wistfulness; when some small part of her wishes it wasn't so, why, we're always there to scream, in those moments, to make our demands that he seek and find the bad. So our Clever Ones seek the bad for us, and they do it well, and they die, in the end, with their heart disease and failing lungs, with alcohol-related liver damage, leaving behind more than one spouse and children who never knew about those moments…those moments when the Clever Ones wished it wasn't so.

Some attorneys are not dismayed by our single-minded drive to punish our enemy. They're full of confidence. They'll soothe us, they're sure, and help us find a way to move on, to restore balance, to make things just. We're hurting, and we're upset—they understand. But there's the Law, you see. And with the help of the Law, Right and Balance can be restored. All will be well, and they're happy to help.

We teach them quickly that we don't want Right, and we don't want Balance. We want our enemy destroyed. And after a while, after "a word" from a senior partner, or when business has been too slow for too long, they begin to steel themselves for what they know they must do. Grim, but determined, they begin to accede to our demands. They become good at finding—or creating—the bad. They comfort themselves with the knowledge that their children *do* know them and love them, and their sensible spouses remain with them, staunchly loyal, and they learn to live with the heaviness of spirit.

We never consider what it costs our attorneys to find the bad for us. They're well paid for their efforts, we remark resentfully, thinking only of the checks we write. We don't think of the other cost, the cost they bear for destroying our enemy. We don't think of their hopes for and disappointment in their fellow man—in themselves! We don't know that when they first met us—even after all they'd seen—a part of them, that faraway, quiet part, searched *our* faces in hopes of finding evidence of the good.

To gain the world and lose your soul is your own business. It is another matter altogether to ask a man to do so on your behalf.

• • • • •

I married an attorney. A young prosecutor, in fact. In all the world, you will find no more honorable men than young prosecutors. Determined to fight the good fight, they're going to put criminals in jail and protect good citizens from harm. And with the help of their brothers in law enforcement, they do it. They lament an occasional bad turn, but they believe in justice and honor, and by and large, they'll tell you with a wide grin, the system works.

After a while, after a long while, the young prosecutors come to understand that they can't put braces on their children's teeth or send them to college on a prosecutor's salary. It's too bad, they'll say, for they love the work, but it *is* taxpayers' money, after all. So for the family's sake, they decide to enter civil practice. They assure their anxious wives that it will be just fine. Time to settle down anyway and stop playing cops and robbers. Time to help folks out a little.

I was thinking of these things as I sat across from my husband in a small coffeehouse one Friday evening, waiting for the evening's entertainment, thinking of the young prosecutor I had married and the quiet stranger who sat across from me now.

When the Sightings began, I tried to explain them to my husband. He did not understand, we argued, and I vowed never to speak of them again. I should not have been surprised that things ended badly; for some time it had been apparent that my husband and I were developing very different ideas about God. Just as I was becoming convinced that God was personal, available, present, my husband, on the other hand, was becoming convinced that God, if He existed at all, was not personal or available. At my cries of protest, he would merely shrug. "A man does the best he can," he'd say, "and I guess there'll be a reckoning at the end."

Like a judge, I'd think, looking at him. *You're here to try your case to the best of your ability, and then when you're done, the judge will make his ruling.*

The last argument that ensued after I tried to express the shift in perception I was experiencing ended abruptly when my husband, uncharacteristically unkind, cried out, "People like me live in the real world, Kelly, so that people like you don't have to."

I was stunned. And mortified.

But the Sightings continued. And we grew further apart.

Sitting there that night with a heavy heart, thinking over all these things, I looked absently about the coffeehouse and spotted a young boy moving about the tables. He was short and squat and his head was shaved. *Oh my goodness!* I thought with amusement. *He looks like a little Buddha!* The boy held my attention, and as I watched him, he stopped at a table and spoke with the people there. After a short while he moved away and stopped at another table, engaging the people there in conversation. He moved slowly from table to table like a little host. I tried to figure out to whom he belonged, but no one seemed to be watching over him like a parent would—and he was only six or seven! As I watched, invariably the people at the table would smile or laugh and appear to be very interested in what the little Buddha had to say. Sometimes, as he left, they would exchange strange glances.

As the boy worked his way closer and closer to our table, I got a better look at his face—wide like his body, scrubbed clean with pink cheeks and pink lips. He had dimples, and his eyes even crinkled at the corners when he smiled, which was often. *Yep. A little Buddha for certain,* I thought, my mood lightening as I watched him.

As the boy moved from the table beside us to the table behind us, I heard the woman at the table next to ours murmur something to her husband. I was sure I heard the words "…something wrong with him." I turned to look at them, and I saw disapproval on the woman's face and her husband's as well. Her husband answered her in an impatient tone, "I wonder where the hell his parents are, letting him roam all over like that."

This surprised me. *Is something wrong with the little Buddha?* I wondered. I turned in my chair in order to better see him at the table behind us, but there was no need, for it was finally our turn for a visit. The boy lumbered up to our table, spread his legs wide apart for support, and lay his chubby little hands, palms down, on our table. I could feel something almost palpable emanating from his fat little body, and his face seemed to shine in the light. He looked first at me, eyes large and green, and I felt a jolt of electricity run through me. The boy looked at me, gaze steady, but he did not speak. I felt a stillness come over me as well, felt as if I had been *asked* to be silent. And so I did not speak. At least not out loud. In my head, I said simply, *Hello, Father.* The boy smiled at me, as if he had heard my unspoken greeting, and then turned to my husband.

I watched them, the little Buddha and my husband, as each returned the other's regard. To my surprise, my husband also remained silent. As they continued to look at each other, not speaking, my heart began to pound.

After a long while, my husband said simply, voice calm and low, "Hi there."

"Hello," answered the boy.

They began to speak quietly then, the two of them, and I sat and watched, amazed. Amazed at the change in my husband's demeanor. There was a softening in his expression, an easing of his tight body posture. They spoke first about the drums on display in the coffeehouse, drums made just as they were made long ago, with only the earth as a resource. They spoke not as man and child, but as two equals. Calmly, quietly, with respect. The boy was obviously very intelligent. *Why had the woman thought something was wrong with him?* I wondered. I don't know what else my husband and the little Buddha said that night, because I stopped listening. Time Stood Still as the silence I felt at the boy's arrival engulfed me, and I sat in a world without sound, watching my husband relax and become kind and gentle in God's presence.

As if on cue, suddenly they were done. The boy turned to me and smiled. "Bye," he said, raising his chubby little hand, fingers spread wide.

"Goodbye," I said quietly.

The spell broke as God's mother came forward from the back of the coffeehouse to call to Him that it was time to go home. "Oh, I want to stay!" God called out, and gentle laughter rippled through the coffeehouse. God laughed too and ran to His mother, throwing His arms around her in a hug. She smiled at the force of His hug and patted His head.

"Maybe next time," she said.

I slowly returned my gaze to the table and stared at my coffee mug until I had fully checked my tears. When I was certain I had my emotions under control, I raised my eyes to my husband's face.

"That was God, you know," my husband said simply, his expression still kind, his eyes regarding me thoughtfully, and Time Stood Still for a second time that night as I saw before me, fully revealed, all the Good I had once seen in the young prosecutor I'd married. It was still there! The tears returned to spill down my cheeks.

"Oh yes! Yes! It was!" I said, reaching to take the outstretched hand he offered me. "It really was!"

Sighting Twenty-One
GOD IS A GREENBELT

I love to think of nature as an unlimited
broadcasting station,
through which God speaks to us every hour,
if we will only tune in.

GEORGE WASHINGTON CARVER

I-I...HATE-YOU. I-I...HATE-YOU. I-I...HATE-YOU.

I sounded the words in my head like a litany to match the rhythm of my feet as they struck the pavement. I began to breathe to the rhythm as well, pulling the air into my lungs and filling them for *I-I*, then expelling it in a whoosh on *hate you*. In and out, in and out, I was one with the rhythm of my hate. Finally, it was not enough just to think it; I began to say it, out loud.

"I-I...hate you."

*I hate you. You don't count. You're not real. I've **seen** real. You're not it. You're just a crappy wannabe. My God, I can see the damn houses behind you!*

It's true. I was cursing trees.

We'd moved from rural Ohio to Houston, Texas, in the middle of the summer. The community we moved into proudly billed itself as "The Livable Forest," and my husband, who had gone to Houston ahead of us to begin work and arrange for our new home, chose a house in that community *because* of the trees, hoping I would be pleased.

I was *not* pleased.

The trees in The Livable Forest were not at all like my beloved trees back home in Ohio. In fact, *nothing* in Houston was like back home, and it was so much more than the trees that I was cursing. I hated everything about our new life. I had traded small for big, slow for fast, wide-open spaces for neighbors on top of one another. I had exchanged the only white two-story house with black shutters on the street, its three-quarter-acre lot, and a view of the lake from its position on top of the hill, for a two-story brick house with a postage-stamp-sized yard. It looked so much like every other two-story brick house on the street that *weeks* after the move, my children were still crying out from the back seat, "Mom! You just drove past our house…*again*."

My favorite perennials could not survive in the Texas heat, and I had abandoned my beautiful deciduous trees for tall scrappy pines that never stopped shedding ugly brown needles on my tiny yard. I had traded fertile, fresh springs, crisp, color-filled falls and snow-filled, snowed-in winters for the never-ending monotony of slightly different versions of the same season. Life was to be forever and always summer now.

Deeper yet, I had traded my lifetime home, the nearness of my family and dearest friends for…for what? So my husband could work a big job in a big city. Feeling perpetually a stranger in a strange land, I quickly forgot that I had agreed to the move, and soon my husband's name began to appear on the list of things I hated.

I left my two-story brick house every morning to run on the greenbelt trails, an old habit from home that I brought with me, along with my antiques, my Blue Willow china, and the box of college books marked "Mom's stuff." Back home in Ohio, I started every day with an early morning walk, or run, and as I'd breathe in the fresh morning air, I could get my thoughts in order, plan for my day, and maybe think about God a little. Being outside soothed me, settled me. But *here*, I'd no sooner hit the greenbelt than my list of hates would appear before me; and the list would consume me until it was all I could think about the entire run. I would look at the trees on either side of the sidewalk and I would think how different they were from the trees at home. Occasionally I'd pass people, but never the same faces, and I'd think of the folks at home

I would be passing if I were there—the woman on the porch, the old couple walking slowly, holding hands, maybe Karita Jo waving on her way to the market for a jug of milk. Why, I could *count* on it. They'd be there and I'd be there and the world would feel as if everything were just as it should be.

And there was something else.

There was something else here that was not the same, and it was the worst of all. It was God. I hadn't seen Him since the move. I couldn't understand it. When I'd meet people here, I'd look at their eyes to try and see God twinkling back at me, or watch to see if they would look up unexpectedly and smile that certain way, maybe say something cryptic that was the signal, between God and me, that it was Him. I'd wait to feel The Shift and the *knowing* that it was God. But it just never came.

God doesn't live in Texas, I'd remark mournfully to the trees. *And I don't blame Him.* A sorrowful feeling would wash over me then, and a feeling of hopelessness. After a while, I began to doubt that the Sightings had ever happened.

I-I…hate yo—

I stopped chanting my litany as I spotted a small girl and her grandfather up ahead of me. As I approached them, they heard the thud of my feet and moved to the side to let me pass. The grandfather was tall and broad-shouldered, and his body moved fluidly.

His hair, although white, was still thick. I could see well-formed calf muscles in his legs as he stepped aside. *Quite fit for a grand-father*, I thought, as I drew nearer. The little girl at his side wore pigtails, placed high on her head but falling to well past her shoulders, and they bounced and floated and moved as if they had a life of their own. The girl's limbs were plump and so was her face. She was the picture of health. Or rather, what we used to call healthy before we became so frightened about our children's weight. She wore glasses, despite her young age, and the lenses were very thick. They magnified the dark-brown eyes that peeped up at me as I trudged by. As she looked at me like that, all pigtails and huge eyes and pink cheeks, I thought dully that there was a time when a girl like that, with eyes like that, would melt my heart.

But not today.

I forced a smile and a curt nod. It was all I could manage.

I plodded on for some seconds, the heaviness of homesickness still upon me, when I heard a soft shuffling noise. I glanced back over my shoulder to discover that the little girl was running behind me. I smiled in spite of myself.

"Hi, honey," I ventured, slowing my stride just a bit.

The girl simply smiled and took her place by my side, the dark eyes intent behind the lenses, the gaze direct and—*probing?* I had the strangest feeling, looking into those eyes, that I was being asked a question. *Ah well, perhaps she's wondering if I'm "nice" or "safe,"* I thought, forcing another smile to reassure her.

A few seconds passed and I expected her to stop, or her grandfather to call her back, but the girl doggedly kept running. I felt inexplicably moved by the child who held her position at my side, yet my sense of homesickness and sorrow felt strangely amplified in her presence as well, so much so that, overwhelmed by it, I found myself unable to speak to her.

"I like to run," she remarked finally.

Speak to her, damn it! I ordered myself sternly. *The child is running with you, for God's sake.*

"Well, that's just great," I responded after an awkward pause. "Running is good for you."

She nodded her assent.

Looking down at her, I noticed that her shoe was untied.

My mother's impulse, reflexive from years of practice, sprang forth automatically. "Oh, honey," I said quickly, stopping. "Your shoe's untied. May I tie it for you?"

She stopped and stuck her foot out. "Yes."

I crouched down at her feet, picked up the laces, and stole a look at her pretty pink face before beginning to tie the shoe. Her eyes readily met mine again, those eyes with their unspoken question. What was the child wondering, looking at me like that?

Her grandfather joined me as I tied the shoe. "Shoe untied again?" he asked, laughing.

"Well, she's just letting me feel good," I responded, looking up into dark eyes still carefully watching me. "Letting me help a little." I smiled at her and offered, "My little girl is older now, and I don't get to tie her shoes anymore. Sometimes I miss that." The girl continued to watch me, her warm hand resting on my shoulder as I finished a double knot. There was something about her hand, resting there, and the way she was watching my face. A feeling of being near something familiar washed over me. *Guess she reminds me of Molly*, I thought, thinking of my own young daughter. Shoe tied, I remained on my haunches a moment longer to look up at her and puzzle over what it was that felt so familiar, so comforting about the child. Returning my regard, she smiled before gently removing her hand.

I stood up, prepared for our goodbyes. "There you go," I said brightly to the girl. And then, "Have a good one," to the grandfather.

But to my surprise, after I'd resumed my run for a short distance, I again heard the soft shuffle-shuffle-shuffle. I turned to see her behind me, and I laughed this time and slowed all the way down to her pace. "It's nice of you to run with me," I offered. As the girl looked up at me, something in me began to soften, and the heaviness in my chest began to dissipate. I felt…lighter.

We ran, she and I, until I began to wonder why her grandfather had not called out for her to stop. Looking back over my shoulder, I was to receive my second surprise. There he was, the grandfather, running himself. He moved slow and steady, maintaining a respectful distance behind but keeping pace, allowing the girl and me to run together. I felt an impulse of concern, but a quick glance at his face immediately reassured me that the jogging was not physically difficult for him. He was comfortable, and he was doing it for her…for me…*for us.*

Touched by his act, I continued on. And for a while, I felt as if Time were standing still. We ran slowly, the girl and I, as if we had all the time in the world. We did not speak, but sometimes I would turn my head to smile down at her, only to find her smiling back up at me. A part of me felt as if I would like nothing more than to just continue running forever, the beautiful little girl at my side, the strong grandfather watching over us from a short distance behind.

But as we approached a section of the greenbelt that opened onto a busy street, my mother's reflex surfaced again and I explained to the girl, "We'll have to stop at the street. Your grandpa wouldn't want you to cross that with me."

"I know," she said simply.

A few steps more, and we stopped.

Looking down at her, I knew we were done. I wasn't sure how I knew, but I knew.

"Th—Thank you for running with me," I said, as I waited for Grandfather to traverse the small distance he had kept so respectfully between us.

"Yes," she answered.

"Thank you, too," I said to Grandfather.

He only smiled and raised his hand in farewell, and she did too, and I crossed the street by myself, stepped back into the greenbelt…and promptly began to cry.

I wasn't even sure why I was crying. I simply knew that I had been touched by their presence. I looked back from my side of the street and caught a glimpse of them through the trees, walking away now, hand in hand. Watching the girl's pigtails bounce, it came over me, slow and easy, as if slow and easy were all I could handle this day.

God.

God…was that You? I asked, wondering. And then it was fully upon me, and I couldn't believe I had missed it. After all those long, lonely weeks, the knowing was upon me again. It all flooded over me, the girl, her willing company, her probing gaze—*God!* Grandfather's respectful distance, his willingness to let the girl accompany me—*God!* How had I not seen it?

I allowed it to wash over me, allowed myself to think about it for a while as I walked slowly along the greenbelt, until finally I sighed, *Oh, God, imagine You coming to me here, here in this place where I have screamed my hate at You every day for all these weeks. Here. This place of hate.*

The soft and gentle feeling of God's presence was lingering around me still, even though the girl and the Grandfather were long gone. Musing about this, I absently raised my eyes up to the tall pine trees above me and to the blue sky behind them—

And I realized suddenly that God wasn't just the girl, or the grandfather.

God was the Greenbelt.

And the Greenbelt had let me pass through it every day and spew my hate and my homesickness and my sorrow all over it and in exchange had simply been…lovingly present. Yes, God was the Greenbelt. I just hadn't noticed because I had been so busy with my hate list. And just as I was beginning to feel that my hate was going to consume me, God made things a little more…*personal.* He sent a pink-cheeked little girl and her handsome grandfather to run with me, to interrupt my hating just long enough to notice *Him.* And now that I had stopped hating, I *did* notice Him—right here, on the Greenbelt. *As* the Greenbelt.

I looked at the trees and vines and palms that were on either side of me now with sudden affection and gratitude; I looked farther up to the small thatches of needles and pinecones at the very tops of the trees. I could almost *feel* the trees loving me back, feel *God* loving me back.

• • • • •

I visit the Greenbelt as often as I can now, the Greenbelt in The Livable Forest with its pine trees, shade trees, and wildflowers, its rabbits, lizards, squirrels, and sometimes deer. I hold Ohio in my heart, but there is room for Houston now, too. It's beautiful. I'm not sure how I missed it all before.

God lives in Texas, my friends.

And who can blame Him?

Sighting Twenty-Two
GOD STUDIES PHILOSOPHY

There are more things in heaven and earth, Horatio,
than are dreamt of in your philosophy.

WILLIAM SHAKESPEARE

AS I SAT, STUNNED, in my large empty house, I knew that I would have to "do" something. The pale walls of the house stared back at me, silently questioning. We sat there, the house and I, listening. There were no noises, no giggles. No suspicious thumps. No sudden shouts. There was nothing, nothing at all. I had the strangest notion that the house was sad. We were sad together. *Everyone leaves*, I thought mournfully. *Everyone always leaves*. Despite their promises to "not grow up" and "stay with Mommy always," the babies were in elementary school. It was more than I could bear, sitting and knowing. Knowing about the leaving. I felt as if the silence—and the sorrow—would consume me, and

I thought to myself, from a far-off place, that I couldn't sit in the silence and loneliness every day. I would go crazy, or break down, or something.

"What should I do?" I whispered to myself and to the listening house, over and over. *What should I do?* What could I do to make the huge Feeling of Emptiness go away? The house seemed to wait expectantly for an answer.

A job? I wondered. Get a job that would take me out of the silent, waiting house? *And just what job would that be?* remarked the cold little voice in my head. *You have no skills. There is nothing you can do.*

The voice was quite right. I was just a mom.

As I sat there, the sunlight shifting and changing across the walls of the room, making them seem like a real, living presence, an idea came over me slowly, working its way through the layers of confusion and sadness. School? Was that it? Was that what I should "do"? Get an education, and when I finally knew enough, get a job? Some kind of job that would keep my mind occupied. The kind of job that keeps you so busy that you don't think about babies, and how they grow up, and how they leave you. And how you think you can't bear the pain when they go.

• • • • •

I sprang into action over the next weeks, spurred by my quiet desperation and my burning desire to escape the silence and loneliness that filled my daytime hours. I made the necessary arrangements to attend a nearby university. Everything fell into place. The paperwork. The loan. The classes. It seemed there was a place for me there. Three days a week, only twenty minutes away from the children. *They still might need me*, I thought hopefully. *They might. You never know.*

Yet despite my happy plans for The Great Escape, the first day of my return to school was overwhelming beyond anything I had imagined. I felt painfully out of place. I was old and they were young. I was dumpy and they were cool and hip. Their backpacks were from JanSport and mine was from Kmart. They knew each other, and I knew no one. But all this, I had expected. What stunned me that day was this: I was stupid, and they were smart. I was mortified. *What were you thinking?* mocked the little voice in my head. *How could you possibly think you belong here?*

I walked into my last class that first day of school deeply shaken and almost late. *Just get through this last class,* I coached myself, *and you never have to come back.* I scanned the room quickly from the doorway at the back of the classroom, and my heart sank as I saw that the only seats left were two in the very front of the room. The aisles were narrow, and I was unaccustomed to moving with a backpack—a backpack crammed with every book for every class, as I had no dorm room to return to between classes and the parking lot for commuters was far away.

Despite my best efforts, as I worked my way to the front of the classroom, I kept knocking my backpack into students who returned only a cool gaze when I apologized. I finally reached the front of the classroom and sat down awkwardly, still struggling with my backpack—*now* the troublesome thing seemed stuck to my back—and, flustered, I couldn't get my arms out from the straps I had tightened at the beginning of the last class in an attempt to alleviate my backache. Finally wrenching my left arm out, I slipped out of it, placing it on the floor. I averted my eyes from the others, looked out the window, and fought back the tears as I waited for class to begin.

I heard a sudden scraping noise and turned around instinctively, as did the others, to see one last student enter through the door in the back. He was huge. Very tall, very broad shouldered, very black. His eyes were large and dark as well—I could see that even from across the classroom. I watched him assess the room confidently, almost defiantly. He strode to the front of the room to take the only seat left…the one in front of me. As I watched him approach, I thought to myself that he must be one of the college athletes, because of his build and his air of self-assurance.

I steeled myself as he approached, telling myself firmly, *You WILL smile and say hi. You have to try.*

As the young man smoothly dropped his coat onto the back of his chair, he assessed the room once more as he stood there, and there was almost a warning, a challenge in his gaze. I kept my shaky smile ready, but he didn't even look at me.

It was the last straw.

You are SO insignificant, the mean little voice in my head remarked coolly, *that he wouldn't even think to look at you...even though you're right here.*

Class began, and as the hour passed I heard little of the philosophy professor's remarks, my energy devoted to maintaining outward composure as I listened to the silent litany of negative self-talk in my mind. My thoughts were interrupted just once, when the professor asked us why we had taken the class. For a minute I allowed myself to imagine, with the sick humor of the quietly desperate, how the professor and the students would react if I raised my hand to answer his question with, "To stop the screaming in my head." And suddenly, the Feeling of Emptiness was upon me again, and the sadness. *Even here,* I thought. *Even in this classroom.* The walls of the classroom became the walls of my house, the sorrow settled like a weight upon my chest, and the whispered, *What should I do? What should I do?* echoed once again in my mind.

I found myself gazing at the broad set of shoulders in front of me. I felt as if I could hide behind them. It was strange, but I could almost feel strength emanating from him. I felt as if it were gently engulfing me. I relaxed a little. I looked out the window some more. My churning thoughts began to quiet, until at the last they became very, very still.

And then, just then, class was over, and I was jolted out of the stillness. My hands began to tremble as I tried to pack my books back into my backpack. The young man in front of me turned around and said, "So. I guess you're what they call a nontraditional student."

It was a statement, not a question, and I mistook the strength in his voice for condescension. Utterly undone by now, I answered in a low voice, with my head down, "Yeah. I guess so."

"So am I." His voice was calm, the tones rich and deep.

I quickly looked up into a broad, smiling face. His dark eyes twinkled. I felt a rush of surprise...confusion...gratitude. *How is he a nontraditional student?* I wondered. *And why is he being nice to ME?* To add to my confusion, the smiling young man seemed to be waiting for me.

I finished loading up my backpack and the young man walked with me out of the building, opening doors for me along the way. We talked very little, but he was kind. I felt better somehow. We parted at the door.

Shortly after I left him, I realized I was lost. Lost on campus. Somewhere along the way, I had turned in the wrong direction. *Oh, my God!* crowed the mean little voice in my head. *You can't even find the parking lot.* Confused by my surroundings, I decided to turn around and retrace my steps. Maybe things would start looking familiar again. As I turned, I looked up and across the street. There he was, sitting on a bench, watching me. Just sitting. And watching. As if he had time…all the time in the world. Even from across the street I could sense a calm and a strength emanating from the young man on the bench. He nodded his head just once and smiled encouragingly.

The rush of embarrassment I experienced at the thought that he had witnessed my mistake was quickly replaced by Something Gentle, Something Reassuring. It was diffusing through me. I could feel it. And that Something seemed connected to him…his nod and his smile…the quiet way he held his body as he sat on the bench.

I smiled back at him and retraced my steps.

I thought about the young man on the drive home. I thought, too, about how much I wanted to learn all the amazing things the smart kids in my classes seemed to already know. I decided to stay in school until the end of the week.

At the next class I arrived almost late once again, and the seat behind the young man was taken. But I still took comfort in watching his broad shoulders from behind. As the class progressed and opinions began to be expressed about the subject matter with that special sort of intensity found only in freshman philosophy classes, the young man spoke up a time or two, making the class laugh with funny little remarks that reminded us to lighten up and not take the subject matter so seriously. Afterward, he waited and walked me all the way to the parking lot—no chance of getting lost this time. He talked quietly about nothing in particular, just life, slipping in little jokes to make me laugh. Walking with him at my side, I decided that school was not so bad after all. I decided that I was going to be okay. I decided not to quit.

I never saw him again.

The young man never returned to class. I never spotted him walking about campus. And I had the funniest feeling that if I asked the other students in the class about him, they wouldn't know who he was, or why he wasn't in class anymore.

It was God. Taking that seat in front of me on my first day, talking to me when no one else would, and watching me from across the way. It was God walking me to my car and talking quietly until the Feeling of Emptiness went away. It was God, staying around just long enough to see to it that I didn't quit school.

Sighting Twenty-Three
GOD IS A DOG

A dog is the only thing on earth that will love
you more than you love yourself.

JOSH BILLINGS

"WE'RE GOING TO GO AROUND THE TABLE," my brother
announced, "and each person will tell something they're grateful for."

I looked up, uneasy. I knew what he was doing. When we
were kids, the ceremonial round-the-table ritual was a family tra-
dition. Birthdays required funny stories about the birthday boy or
girl (*embarrassing* funny stories, of course), New Year's called for
each person's proclamation of their single most important reso-
lution, and the remaining holidays were for listing what we were
grateful for. We were grown and starting families of our own now,
and I knew that my brother had made his announcement, here in
his own house, to try to make me feel comfortable, to try to make

my first holiday away from home special.

Please, no, I thought. I deliberately tightened my stomach muscles to help myself focus on controlling the emotions that were churning inside of me; but like simmering water that begins to rattle the lid of the pot, my emotions continued to boil, to bubble and hiss.

I can't.

I looked first at the adults and then at the children around the long table as the roundabout began. My heart began to pound. How to tell my brother that I was not thankful? How to tell my nieces and my own children that I hated my new home and my new life? That a holiday in this new place did not feel like a holiday, and that I hated that too? How to tell them all that the gratitude statement that first sprang to my mind, colored both by the despair I truly felt as well as the Irishwoman's flair for dramatic expression, was:

Why, I am grateful that I'm even sitting here. That I'm still alive. That I haven't gone stark raving mad or taken my own life. In short, I'm grateful that I haven't yet been consumed by the horror that is my life.

I didn't mean it, really. Or I did.

The children—with eyes toward dessert—had been grateful quickly, and it was already my turn. The emotions were threatening to bubble over, to spill out of the pot, and as I struggled for self-control, tears filled my eyes. I waved my hand at the others at the table, gesturing for them to pass me by, managing only an, "I can't." Looking around the table at their faces, it occurred to me what a sick twist of irony it was that the adults were assuming that I was too overcome with *gratitude* to speak. I felt nauseous. As I watched their tender expressions, knew their sentimental thoughts directed toward me, I thought that I might, after all, lose my mind, right there in front of them all.

My husband's cell phone rang. He stepped out into the hallway to take the call, which was brief, then motioned for me to join him in the hallway. A voice on the other end of the phone had explained to my husband that our beloved lab had been struck by a car traveling at a high rate of speed, and then left dead on the side of a highway ten miles from our home. A heartbroken onlooker had buried her. The voice on the phone had saved her pink collar. Did we want it?

It all played out badly. My husband gave me the news in hushed tones, but his low voice carried and our daughter overheard bits and pieces.

"Mom? Mom? WHAT DID DAD SAY?" She jumped up from her chair and ran to us. "What happened to the dogs? MOM!"

The other three children left their seats and ran into the hallway, surrounding us, and we were forced to tell the children right there, Thanksgiving feast a mere eight feet away, that Ethel had been hit. And died.

There. Was. Pandemonium.

The girls sobbed.

"I want to go home, Mom," my oldest son cried. "Please. Mom. I want to go home."

His little brother picked up the cry and began to wail, "I-I-I-I wanna go hoooooooome."

"We'll leave soon, Son," I replied, wondering which my sister-in-law would find more awkward: our family leaving immediately or after dessert. My stomach knotted at the thought of driving from Austin to Houston with four heartbroken children.

"NO, MOM," my son was insisting, interrupting my thoughts. He reached out to take my hand. "NOT HOUSTON. I want to go home-home. I want to go home to Ohio."

I began to cry then too, wondering if the dogs had been trying to go home to Ohio as well.

We finished our holiday with my brother and then drove back to Houston. The children fell asleep somewhere around Brenham, and I turned to gaze dully out of the window and think of Ethel…

We'd wandered into the local animal shelter on a Saturday afternoon during an open house at the fairgrounds, and there she was, a six-month-old yellow lab in the bottom cage. As my children and other visitors oohed and aahed and giggled over the eight-week-old litter of beagles that had been found abandoned in an alley, and the calico kittens finally ready for adoption, I looked at the lab and thought to myself that her competition was awfully stiff.

The lab seemed to know. She lay in her cage, her chin on the ground between her two front paws, looking up at me, her tail thump-thump-thumping slowly. But she did not get up. She heaved a doggy sigh.

I turned abruptly to my husband. "I don't care what *they* say," I said, pointing to my noisy children. "If we're getting one today, we're getting *her*."

To his curious gaze I could only respond with a shrug as I said, "I can't help it. She doesn't stand a chance."

She came home with us that day, and she became Ethel to our German Shorthaired Pointer, Lucy. My husband and I laughed, thinking how appropriate the names were, for we discovered quickly that Ethel would have gladly spent the day laying in the sun, or at our feet, moving as little as possible, except that there was Lucy. Lucy who was constantly insisting that they had things to *do*. Birds to sneak up on, holes to dig, neighbor dogs to run up and down the fence line with, and on a lucky day, a rabbit to chase and never catch.

Their adventures also included an occasional break for it

should a gate be left open with scolding grownups nowhere in sight. Off they'd go for several hours, making their usual rounds. They wandered freely through the neighborhood of our little lakeside development, then out into the fields, and finally into the woods, only to return, mud-covered, tails wagging, for supper and a bath.

When we moved to our new home in Houston, we worried about what would happen to Lucy and Ethel if they escaped into the new neighborhood with its cars and unfamiliar territory. We worried particularly about Ethel. If Lucy sprinted across a street in the lightning fast way that only a Pointer can bound, we knew Ethel would follow; and while Lucy might beat the traffic, Ethel wouldn't. We became zealous about shutting and locking the gates.

Until now. Until the holidays.

It was exactly what we had feared. The gate latch had been left UP, and the dogs made a break for it. Lucy made it across the road. Ethel didn't.

We pulled into our driveway with heavy hearts. The darkness in my spirit remained, the loss of Ethel one more loss in a series of losses. And even as the tears slipped down my cheeks as we entered the house—a house that *still* did not feel like my home—there was a part of me, the same part of me that had threatened to shock my family at the table, that merely shrugged and said, *But of course. What did you expect?*

• • • • •

I pulled into the driveway one Saturday afternoon, lost in thought, and popped the back hatch of the minivan to grab a bag of groceries. As I approached the front door, still going over my mental checklist, wondering what I had forgotten *this* time, I was startled by a large black dog lying on my front porch. She looked up at my approach and proceeded to unfold her long limbs, stretching and yawning before lumbering toward me, tail wagging.

As I stood there, assessing her for friendliness, the front door flew open and my son, who had been watching for me from the window, came bounding out, shouting, "Mom! Mom! She just followed me home!"

I raised a skeptical eyebrow, and he began to insist.

"Mom. When I left the park, she just followed me. I didn't call to her or anything. Promise. *Really*, she just did it on her own. She followed me the whole way home!"

She followed him home, dirty, underfed, and collarless. On the doorstep sat a large bowl of water and a smaller empty bowl that I assumed had held food prior to my arrival, but I said nothing.

I dropped a hand for her to sniff, and she nuzzled it.

"She can't stay," I told my son firmly. "We'll have to find her owners."

I rubbed her head and noticed that I could see her ribs. I pursed my lips. Word in the neighborhood was that sometimes folks from the next town over dumped unwanted animals off on the greenbelt trails near our park.

I looked down at her only long enough to say, "You can't stay. We'll find your owners."

"Mom," my son pleaded. "No collar!"

"Her family is probably sad and missing her," I countered. "Think how happy they'll be."

He sighed and nodded, before tendering a hopeful, "But, if —"

"No, Son," I said gently. "We just lost Ethel. I can't bear another loss. No more dogs for a while."

My son took the bag of groceries from me. I knew that he hadn't heard a word I'd said, and would be working overtime in the days to come to prove to me that he deserved this dog. *Damn*, I thought.

Both hands free now, the dog nuzzled me again, and I looked down into a pair of loving brown eyes. I was taken aback, looking at those eyes, and it occurred to me that they were the most loving eyes I'd ever seen, animal or man.

Within two hours we had bathed her and invited her into our backyard—to keep her safe, of course, from traffic. Lucy was overjoyed, and the two dogs played together immediately, chasing, jumping, and wrestling. By day's end, she was allowed in the house.

We posted pictures on the streetlamps and in the stores. We contacted the local vet and checked for a microchip. We asked around the neighborhood. I warned the children not to get attached; someone would come for her. I was sure, I told them, with a loving dog like that.

She made the children laugh with the way she'd cock her head when they talked to her, or the funny things that happened as she clumsily maneuvered her big body through the house. Her tail struck the most interesting things. She sounded my crystal singing bowl, knocked over plants, and sometimes I'd walk into the family room to discover one boy rolling on the floor, howling, arms crossed at the wrists and jammed between his closed legs, the other boy convulsing in laughter, shouting, "She got 'im again." At which point *both* boys would erupt into fresh peals of laughter.

And then there was me. She followed me everywhere, laying at my feet when I checked my email, laying on the floor to watch me clean, sleeping curled up at night next to my side of the bed. If I left the room, she followed. If I sat down, she sat down as well, laying her chin on my lap. She would look at me with those eyes, soft and gentle, and I would pet her head. Sometimes, although I would not let myself think about the Why of it, I would feel as if I were going to cry.

Other times, when the children weren't around to see, I threw my arms around her and hugged her. She remained very still. As I held her, it crept over me, slow and easy. I felt as if Something was holding me in return.

Yeah. You're definitely losing it, remarked the cold little voice in my head. *Losing. It.*

I began to dread a phone call that might claim her.

The dread was needless. The call never came. After several weeks, arms wrapped around her neck, I announced to the children that I thought it safe to assume we were keeping her. We named her Joan. (After Joan of Arcadia.)

"Maybe Ethel sent her," I said, petting her head as she looked up at me.

"No, Mom," my son corrected me. "Maybe *God* sent her."

It was my youngest daughter who piped up then and said, "No, Mommy. She *is* God. Look at her eyes."

I *did* look at her eyes, as I asked her, smiling, "Why, Joan, are you God?"

The children giggled as Joan wagged her tail and licked my hand. I finally allowed both my emotions and my understanding to flow. *Of course* God was reaching out to me in a way in which I would allow myself to be reached. Following me around, staying near, offering me Love…and calling Love forth from me in the process.

Sighting Twenty-Four
GOD IS AN ATHEIST

Men are better than their theology.

RALPH WALDO EMERSON

HE LOOKED JUST LIKE A SCIENTIST SHOULD LOOK. He was slight and angular, his appearance impeccable in a white button-down oxford shirt and perfectly sized Levi's jeans—not too tight and not too loose on his slim form. His short hair remained obediently in place and his glasses, lenses spotless, never dared slide down his nose. His coffee never sloshed out of its mug, his steps were never unsure as he paced the stage with animation, and he never misspoke or lost his train of thought, an astounding matter in and of itself, as his rapid flow of words was a clear indicator of racing, multifaceted thoughts. He pretended to shuffle through his notes while waiting for class to begin, but the observant knew they were in perfect order, both in his mind and his hands. When he took the podium at the front of the classroom and addressed the 120-member class, his demeanor conveyed both the cool confidence of Someone Who Knows Many Things, as well as the great excitement of Someone Who Knows Many Things. His voice was crisp and clear, and often, in spite of himself, passionate and enthusiastic.

The Man Who Knew Many Things found those things to be quite amazing, and he wanted his students to understand this as well. Ah! The things the science professor taught his students, those who wanted to listen. He taught about atoms and cells and DNA. About bacteria and viruses. He helped his students understand photosynthesis and taught them how to identify plants. Old science, current science—the professor only wished he had time to teach it all. But, he would tell the class with a sigh, he didn't have it—the time, that is. They were his for only a short while. He'd just have to do the best he could with the time he had, he'd say smoothly, and then he'd tell a story about a brilliant but troubled genius, or a joke at his own expense, before returning to the matter at hand.

There was something else the professor wanted his students to understand. He wanted them to understand that while they were free to believe what they chose, there was no God. No proof anyway, that was certain. Science could explain everything…every single thing. He was sorry if there were creationists in the room, or stouthearted believers—he did not mean to offend—but we were all big boys and girls and we must not be afraid to look at what science was revealing more and more every day. There simply was no God. He was an atheist. He told us so. He was really quite cheerful about it.

He was also cheerful about making himself available to students who had questions. He invited us to stop by his office. He would be there, he assured us, and he welcomed questions. He would take questions before and after class, and he was often surrounded by hoverers.

Good professors can be marked by their hoverers. Hoverers are students who hover nearby before or after class, offering help, engaging the teacher in conversation, asking questions, or simply standing near while others do so. Hoverers hover because they feel welcome to do so. *That* marks a professor as a Teacher.

• • • • •

I missed an important class one day and found, to my dismay as I read through the book, that I was not going to be able to understand the missed material on my own. I complained to a friend and she reminded me that the material was going to be heavily emphasized on the upcoming test. Not understanding the material would mean not passing the test—the professor had made that clear.

I reluctantly approached the professor at the end of the next class, both to explain my absence and mention that I *might* need to stop by his office with a couple of questions on the missed material. I'd take another look at the material and let him know. I was deliberately noncommittal because I was intimidated by the science teacher and all the things the science teacher knew. I dreaded the thought of exposing the full extent of my ignorance to such a brilliant mind and I was still desperately scheming to find some way of understanding the missed material without making an appointment to see him. The professor graciously ignored my obvious discomfort as I shifted nervously from foot to foot and he answered cheerily that I should feel free to stop by after class or during office hours.

By the time I returned to his class the next day, I had decided not to make an appointment to see him. I had decided that it would just be too embarrassing. I'd have to find some other way to understand mitosis and take my chances on the upcoming test. Maybe I'd get lucky. As I was slinking toward the door at the end of class, one in 120, I was stopped dead in my tracks by a familiar crisp, clear voice from behind me.

"Ms. Hanes. You needed to see me." It was a statement really, not a question. I turned around and answered uncomfortably that, yes, I supposed I did.

"I'll see you in my office in ten minutes."

I spent the next ten minutes in the bathroom thinking about how ignorant I was and about how shocked the science teacher was going to be when he found out. My science background was weak; and although I loved everything I was learning in his class, I was always one or two steps behind, straining to catch up with the others.

Finally, I forced myself out of the bathroom, down the hall, and to his door. I knocked and he called for me to enter. He swung around from his computer and motioned to a chair. I slipped my backpack off my shoulder and sat down. He explained that he would be with me in just a moment and returned to his computer. I used the brief wait to look around his office for clues to his out-of-the-classroom personality. *What moves an atheist?* I thought to myself as I looked around curiously. But there were no framed famous quotes on the wall, no meaningful artwork. Just the fresh, clean, white walls. *Just like a scientist's office,* I thought approvingly.

He turned to me and asked simply, "Now, then?"

I nervously dug through my backpack, trying to locate my hastily scribbled list of questions. When I finally found the list, I wasn't sure how to begin. I glanced at him, but he seemed undisturbed by my apparent lack of preparation. He was waiting patiently.

"I probably shouldn't have taken your class," I blurted. "It was too soon. But I do really like it, and I want to try to pass it."

"Latest test score?" he inquired.

Told you, laughed the cold little voice in my head triumphantly. *I told you.*

I shared the score with downcast eyes and lowered tone to express my shame. I had barely passed. He shrugged lightheartedly, remarking cheerfully that many students "barely passed" his first test. I was in good company and was not to worry. "Now, today's questions?"

Resigned to my present course, as well as the embarrassment that would accompany it, I said simply, "It's mitosis. I don't get it." So the professor carefully explained mitosis to me, and when he finished, he asked me if I understood.

I lied. I said yes.

I was far, far too embarrassed to admit that despite his careful explanation, I was still hopelessly lost. I just wanted to thank him and get out.

He looked at me thoughtfully for a minute and said simply, "Let's try this." He opened my textbook to the pages with pictures of mitosis and explained once again, his pencil flying with notes and diagrams across the two pages. When he was done, I understood mitosis. And mitosis was…*amazing*.

I thanked him sincerely and left. At the end of the week, I passed the test with a little more wiggle room than the previous test, and I began to think I might be able to pass the class, if only barely. The class became increasingly more interesting to me and soon became the class that kept me in school. Near semester's end I had to face a shocking fact: I loved science.

One day in class the science teacher became animated about fungi, and my hand was racing across the page as I tried to keep up with my notes. (It was my misfortune that almost everything the science teacher said was new to me and thus needed to be record-ed for future study.) I could barely look up when he lectured; the glance cost me too much time! This day was no different. But when the science teacher paused that day, I cast a quick glance up at the podium, and in stunned amazement, I dropped my pencil.

I could not believe what I was seeing.

There was light, everywhere. And it was emanating from the science teacher. I don't mean just the typical "white light" you hear stories about—although that seemed to be present as well—rather, there was a myriad of colors streaming out from the man at the podium, out into the classroom. Not dark and bold, but soft and pastel. The light seemed to shimmer, to vibrate almost. I literally gasped out loud, and I instinctively turned to look at the students across the aisle to see what they thought. But they seemed to be unaware. Some sat with bored looks on their faces. Some were sleeping. One was inspecting his fingernails. *What is happening?* I thought. I turned to the left—surely they saw? No one seemed to be aware of the light, not even my friend, who looked at me quizzically when she saw the look on my face. *Oh, my God, I'm losing it,* I thought, and my stomach knotted with fear. *I'm truly going crazy.*

I turned my gaze back to the podium.

It was still there. He was there. The light was there. And the light was coming from him. Suddenly, time seemed to stand still, everything seemed frozen. There was no rush. I could feel it. So I sat and looked. And looked. I even had time to inspect the ceiling lights, to ascertain that they were not responsible for what I was seeing. And still the light did not fade. Random pictures seemed to come before my mind's eye as I watched the man and the light. <flash> The hoverers. <flash> The smile on his face when he invited students to stop by his office with questions. <flash> The white, white walls of his office. <flash> His thoughtful look as he said to me, "Let's try this." It slowly came over me, the full understanding of what I was seeing.

Father, I asked in disbelief, but also with a quickening, an excitement, *is that You?*

The light did not fade but seemed to shimmer and intensify.

How can that be? He doesn't even believe in You. He's an atheist.

I couldn't explain it. But God was there, in the professor. Pouring out of him. Flooding the room. I saw it with my own two eyes, and no one will ever convince me I didn't. I wasn't losing my mind—I was gaining my Mind.

God is an atheist teaching students the wonders of His world. Telling stories about brilliant but troubled geniuses and cracking jokes at His own expense. Welcoming the hoverers. Waiting in His office to answer questions. Explaining mitosis.

Present even when we are unaware.

Sighting Twenty-Five
GOD IS A BOY

But Jesus called the children to him and said,
"Let the little children come to me, and do not
hinder them, for the kingdom of God belongs
to such as these. Truly I tell you, anyone who
will not receive the kingdom of God like a
little child will never enter it."

LUKE 18: 16-17

THERE ARE SOME DAYS that come to us filled with such beauty and grace that we ought to know that Something Wonderful is going to happen. But it is only in looking backward, it seems, that we catch ourselves saying, "Oh, my goodness! I should have known…"

• • • • •

The air was cool and fresh with just a hint of the scent of flowers, bees humming, birds chattering, and all the colors so very, very vivid. It was spring, and it was spring with a flourish. We lived in a huge, rambling, turn-of-the-century home complete with a picket fence, carriage house, and chicken coop now converted into a shed. The old girl needed work, but I didn't mind. We painted her in an authentic four-color Victorian scheme, and there'd be time enough for the rest, I figured, when the children were older. Besides, she was beautiful *now*, I thought this day, as I looked up at her from my place on the sidewalk, admiring her full front porch with its pillars and decorative spindles, her original windows, surrounded by green, green grass and last year's perennials showing such promise. I'd never seen her look so beautiful. I'd never seen a day so beautiful.

• • • • •

The local preschool operated in the basement of a small church just around the corner from our house, and walking my four-year-old son home was one of the best parts of my day, him chattering, me loving, and both of us feeling as if we had time…all the time in the world.

My son had received his first "baseball" haircut. Looking down at his little head, I felt a spasm of love pass through my heart this beautiful spring day, and as I rested my hand gently on his precious head, rubbing it gently back and forth across his burr haircut, a thought suddenly came to me. *Why, I would have come…just for this*. I would have said yes to a sometimes painful human existence just for that, just for that moment. To be his mother on a spring day, my hand resting on his head. I will never forget that day. I will never forget that moment.

My tender musings were abruptly interrupted by the raucous shouts of a little girl. She had rolled down the front passenger's window of a car parked along the sidewalk to lean out and call to my son, "Hey, baldie! Baldie! Baldie! Baldie! You look bald! Your hair looks ugly. *You're* ugly."

Stunned, I looked up to see the little girl hanging out of the car window, her cheeks pink with exertion, her blond piggytails moving slightly in the breeze. My young mother's heart was deeply wounded as I listened to her taunt my sweet and gentle son.

"Oh, son!" I gasped. "That horrible girl! That bad girl—"

I looked down at him, and my exclamation stopped mid-sentence as I, stricken, watched *him* looking at *her*. I watched first bewilderment, then pain pass over his round little face before he became very still, his expression deeply thoughtful, his eyes never leaving her face.

Tears sprang to my eyes, watching him look at her like that, and I rushed on, saying, "That rude, rude girl. You mustn't listen to her, son. She's just being mean. I don't know how she could be so mean. And *her mother*! How can she—"

He turned his steady gaze from the girl to me, looked me straight in the eyes, and said simply, "Don't worry, Mommy. I know her. Her didn't mean it."

Ah, my son! I cried out in my mind, feeling as if my heart would break into a million pieces. *This world will eat you alive.*

But he was regarding me intently just now, his large hazel eyes clear and penetrating, his expression sure and strong. He smiled as he reached out to pat my arm reassuringly. "Don't worry, Mommy," he gently coached me again. "It's *okay*. I *KNOW* her. Her didn't mean it."

Looking into his eyes, watching the lights in them shift and change, I felt something very still move over me. I understood in a way that even now I cannot fully express, that I was in the presence of something very profound, something very holy.

On that day, on that holy day, God taught me how to respond to every attack, every insult, and every unkindness that I will ever experience. The image of the round-faced little boy with the burr haircut and steady hazel eyes with their shifting lights is ever before me, his quiet, confident words ever echoing in my mind. And when all else fails, when I'm having trouble "forgiving" someone, I repeat my son's words to myself, over and over like a litany, "It's *okay*. I *Know* her. Her didn't mean it."

On that day God was trying to teach me that we never really

do mean it. It is not our True Nature to wound, to attack, to hurt. And when we do, it is because we have forgotten our True Nature. When a brother strikes us, what God asks of us—*all* God asks of us—is that we remember our brother's True Nature—that we *Know* our brother, the real him, the only part of him that truly matters... the part of him that is God's.

Sighting Twenty-Six
GOD IS A MEAN WOMAN

We must learn to reawaken and keep ourselves
awake, not by mechanical aid,
but by an infinite expectation of the dawn.

HENRY DAVID THOREAU

THE BOY WAS TO RETURN SIX YEARS LATER to finish what he had started on that fine spring day.

Is it true? I sat wondering one morning. *Are we extensions of God?* How could that be possible? We are so awful to one another, we do such horrible things. How could extensions of God do the things we do? *Children* of God, perhaps—and many of us bad children at that—but *extensions* of God Himself? It seemed too much. I closed the book I had been reading, feeling uneasy. Still mulling over what I had read, I walked into the family room where my four children were watching cartoons. I stopped and stood in the doorway for a moment, unseen, watching the four little lights of my life. And again I whispered to myself, *Can it be true? Can it possibly be true?*

On impulse, I moved through the room, dropping a kiss on each head or cheek before looking into the eyes turned to me and saying softly, "Hi, God." There was no surprise, no questioning. After all, Mommy often said or did strange things after her "quiet time" in the front room. Each child returned an easy smile, or a "Hi," and that was the end of it.

A few days later, I drew a picture—for them and for me—of people as extensions of God. They giggled at my poor artwork, my big "blob" in the middle of the page that extended out in five places to form poorly drawn figures, each with a name on its chest, representing each one of us. Artwork aside, I asked them, laughing myself, "What do you think?"

There was only a moment's pause while they considered it. Why, it seemed "just right," they told me, just like it should be.

And I wondered again at the possibility of that word "extension."

A week later, I woke up on the wrong side of the bed. I felt irritable. Everything that could go wrong did. Despite denying it when asked the night before if they had homework, the twins suddenly "remembered" at the breakfast table that they had work undone. My ten-year-old announced that he didn't have any paper for school. Admonishing all of them to finish breakfast quickly and get dressed for school—and the twins to finish their homework!—I drove quickly to the nearby market to purchase a tablet of paper, only to be informed upon my return, complete with dejected expression and heavy sigh, that it wasn't the "right" kind of paper. The house was a wreck, the laundry was piled sky high, and I— well, I was a mean woman. I ranted. I raved. I scolded. I stomped. I slammed.

When it came time for the children to leave for the bus, I sat muttering at the kitchen table, shuffling through bills and neglected paperwork. Each child ran over to me and kissed my cheek. Looking at their dear little faces, something in me began to soften. That they would still approach me with such love after the fit I had thrown! I heard the door slam as they left the house, and I sat staring miserably at the paperwork in front of me.

I heard the front door open and close again, and looking up, I found my ten-year-old standing in the doorway. Grinning, he stood there just long enough to say, "Bye, God."

I was stunned. Forever stunned. I have never stopped being stunned, and I have never been the same.

I began to cry with remorse for my behavior, begging God for what I was sure was the 9,999th time to help me "do better," when suddenly the Sightings began to flood my mind, all of them seemingly simultaneously, accompanied by every thought they had evoked, every insight gained, every realization they had effected. Lost in what was happening to me, I stopped crying and a slow, easy calm began to creep over me.

I finally understood that it was God who had dropped those gentle kisses on my cheek, and it was God who had stood in my doorway. There God stood, looking right at me, *grinning* at me, letting me know that I'd given Him my very worst and it hadn't affected His opinion of me in the slightest. There He stood, gently laughing, letting me know that the only part of me that mattered, the only part of me that was Real to Him was the part of me that was *His*. It was as if the other things didn't even exist.

It was my final lesson, although it is a lesson I am required to repeat time and time again. It does not matter. It is a lesson I am determined to repeat until I know it so well that I will never, ever forget again.

There is, after all, nowhere He is not.

Conclusion
IT BEGINS

I didn't come here to tell you how this is going to end.
I came here to tell you how it's going to begin.

NEO, *THE MATRIX*

AND NOW YOU BEGIN TO SEE that there is nowhere God is not. He is the boy in his pajamas standing next to your bed as you wake up, asking for Cheerios. He is the little girl singing softly to herself as she brushes her doll's hair. He is the old lady moving slowly down the street using a walker and trying to walk her beloved dog at the same time. He is the coworker across the conference table, the doctor entering the examining room, the secretary who asks if you're sure you're all right today. He is the cashier at the store who remarks that it's going to be a scorcher. He's the man who tells you your brake pads are shot.

Every face you pass at the mall—He is there. All those families at the amusement park—He is there. See Him in Father's smiling face as he holds his daughter's hand. Hear Him in Mother's easy laugh as she scoops up the toddler dashing gleefully to his escape. See Him in the coach who tells boys in pants too long and helmets too big to "hold the bat like this," or demands that his teenagers "play clean." See Him in the teacher as she looks steadfastly at her class, telling them, "Only *you* can choose who you want to be." See Him in Grandfather sitting quietly in his chair.

See Him in the teenagers with baggy clothes, long hair, skateboards, and trick bikes. See Him in the man in the business suit, hustling down the street as if he's late for a meeting. See Him in the poor man on the corner holding a sign that says "Wasn't Expecting This."

See Him. See Him. See Him. There is nowhere He is not.

Epilogue to God Is a Sick Girl
SOMETHING WONDERFUL

THE NEWS WAS GRIM after the ten-hour surgery. It was cancer, as expected, the doctors explained, and it was far more invasive than they had expected. The tumor had wrapped itself around the brainstem, twisting it to the side, and its ugly fingers were threaded all through her brain. The doctors had been able to remove "almost all" of the cancer, but some was left behind because it was growing in such a sensitive area of the brain—too risky, the doctors felt, to try to remove it. They were hoping the chemotherapy and radiation would kill it.

As it turned out, the young girl had moved many hearts. The children in her school brought in gifts, made cards, and prayed for her in their churches. The grownups sent money in with the children and activated prayer chains. The nurses fluttered about her, calling her a little angel.

And somehow, Something Wonderful began to happen…

One day after the surgery, an MRI revealed that the cancer was no longer there. Anywhere.

Three days after the surgery, the doctors met with the girl's mother to apologize. They were so sorry. They were experienced surgeons and they were seldom wrong. There had been no doubt in their minds that what they were removing from Emily's brain was cancer. But the second biopsy results were back, and they had checked and double-checked with the boys in the lab. They wanted to apologize for scaring them. Because it wasn't. It wasn't cancer. It just wasn't.

Young Emily need only heal from the surgery now. There would be no chemotherapy, no radiation, no preparing for "the worst." They couldn't explain it.

It was, the doctors agreed, Something Wonderful.

About the Author
KELLY HANES

Born and raised in small-town Ohio and shaped by big-city Houston, Kelly Hanes enjoys running on the greenbelt trails with her boxer Sophia, binge-watching Netflix series, and saying "yes" to experiences that make her introvert self gasp.

She has a BA in English with a focus on creative writing from the University of Houston and received the Outstanding Thesis for 2011 Award from The Honors College for her thesis, "Wordsworth and the Religious Experience."

Kelly blogs at www.kellyhanes.com, where she writes about the inspiration we can find in our everyday lives.

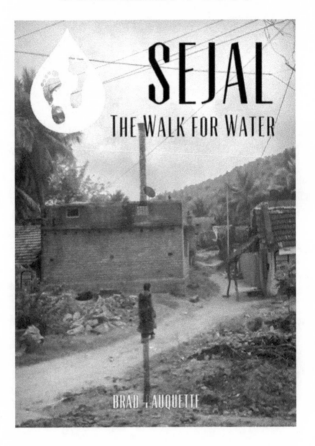